T0312695

Praise for *The Opportunity Index*

"I've never been more desperately eager to endorse a book, yet I have never found it harder to write or articulate the actual endorsement. And there is a good reason for this: *The Opportunity Index* is such a multifaceted, intellectually robust yet curious, meticulously well researched, historically in-depth, culturally rich, and refreshingly written book that it is painfully hard to do it the justice it truly deserves.

"Case in point, from an ethnic diversity angle, there is scarcely an area in global industry that is more worthy of deep dive examination than Britain's and America's financial sectors. These are places that owe much of their origins and wealth to the transatlantic slave trade. They are the epicenter of the racial wealth gap. And like many of the monuments to British and American greatness and success in industry, politics, and religiosity, the City of London and Wall Street are both fascinatingly grandiose yet opaque places. If you come from a working-class background, the construction of the buildings, dress codes, professional conduct, language, and unwritten rules can be enormous barriers to entry. And even greater barriers to prosperity lie within. Yet when compared to other areas in British and American industry, especially liberal-dominated areas such as media, arts, and culture, the City, Wall Street, and the broader financial sectors have done a much better job of providing opportunities—indeed life-changingly lucrative opportunities—to people traditionally shut out of major industry. Very far from a utopia, the City and Wall Street have created once inconceivable professional openings for working-class children of Black immigrants and the descendants of slaves such as Gavin.

"I personally could not think of anyone better placed to conduct this examination of the racial wealth gap and offer solutions than Gavin Lewis, a person who works and lives at the heart of the juxtaposition of opportunity and historical oppression. Despite the might of the challenge, in *The Opportunity Index* Gavin has created a work of true public service that can conclusively transform how we view, discuss, and address diversity, representation, access to opportunity, and closing the racial wealth gap, a term this book should help make greater common currency in socioeconomic and political discussions and decisions.

"By looking back and taking us on a journey of our histories as people and his own unique history as a working-class Black man who grew up in the economically challenged inner-city area of London to a captain of the finance industry as well as observing the shortcomings of the education and political systems and economic orthodoxy, Gavin shows us how we arrived at the challenge we currently face, and the magnitude of that challenge. Yet by looking so far forward into a potentially much brighter future and offering robust solutions as to how we get there, *The Opportunity Index* helps us pave the path to the more egalitarian, meritocratic, and wholesome tomorrow that we all yearn for."

—**Nels Abbey**, writer, broadcaster, and founder of the Black Writers Guild

"The discussions regarding racism, discrimination, and inequity are incredibly important in order to challenge harmful stereotypes many communities fight against. Importantly, they lift the lid on the divisions within the societies we hope would be structured on meritocracy and they provoke debates which cause us to ask ourselves: what can we do? The difficulty with many of these conversations is that they spend a lot of resources and energy focused on the trauma caused by discrimination, but not enough on what needs to be done to disrupt the catalysts which cause that trauma to exist, or at least allows it to continue. *The Opportunity Index,* with the powerful personal perspectives of the author, allows the reader to fully understand the various ways that race can be a direct barrier to wealth and its creation. This context frames the basis of the solutions that present a direct challenge to the status quo and misconception that the solution to racism sits with those who are treated differently because of the amount of melanin in their skin. The book focuses on presenting an objective way of assessing the impact racial advantage has in the same way many would assume simply a good education would. The complexity of creating equal societies is tackled brilliantly by Gavin and is a must read for those who want future generations, essentially my children and their own, not to have to be held to any different standards. *The Opportunity Index* doesn't lift the lid on what causes racial discrimination (many have focused on that for years), but instead focuses on the hope left in Pandora's box with an optimism for how we move forward in tackling inequality, institutional cultural bias, and planning for a world where there is a higher standard than simply the absence of discrimination being celebrated."

—**Tim Campbell,** MBE, BBC's *The Apprentice*

THE
OPPORTUNITY
INDEX

GAVIN LEWIS

THE

OPPORTUNITY

INDEX

A SOLUTION-BASED

FRAMEWORK TO

DISMANTLE

THE

RACIAL WEALTH GAP

WILEY

Copyright © 2023 by John Wiley & Sons, Inc. All rights reserved.

Published by John Wiley & Sons, Inc., Hoboken, New Jersey.
Published simultaneously in Canada.

No part of this publication may be reproduced, stored in a retrieval system, or transmitted in any form or by any means, electronic, mechanical, photocopying, recording, scanning, or otherwise, except as permitted under Section 107 or 108 of the 1976 United States Copyright Act, without either the prior written permission of the Publisher, or authorization through payment of the appropriate per-copy fee to the Copyright Clearance Center, Inc., 222 Rosewood Drive, Danvers, MA 01923, (978) 750-8400, fax (978) 750-4470, or on the web at www.copyright.com. Requests to the Publisher for permission should be addressed to the Permissions Department, John Wiley & Sons, Inc., 111 River Street, Hoboken, NJ 07030, (201) 748-6011, fax (201) 748-6008, or online at http://www.wiley.com/go/permission.

Trademarks: Wiley and the Wiley logo are trademarks or registered trademarks of John Wiley & Sons, Inc. and/or its affiliates in the United States and other countries and may not be used without written permission. All other trademarks are the property of their respective owners. John Wiley & Sons, Inc. is not associated with any product or vendor mentioned in this book.

Limit of Liability/Disclaimer of Warranty: While the publisher and author have used their best efforts in preparing this book, they make no representations or warranties with respect to the accuracy or completeness of the contents of this book and specifically disclaim any implied warranties of merchantability or fitness for a particular purpose. No warranty may be created or extended by sales representatives or written sales materials. The advice and strategies contained herein may not be suitable for your situation. You should consult with a professional where appropriate. Further, readers should be aware that websites listed in this work may have changed or disappeared between when this work was written and when it is read. Neither the publisher nor authors shall be liable for any loss of profit or any other commercial damages, including but not limited to special, incidental, consequential, or other damages.

For general information on our other products and services or for technical support, please contact our Customer Care Department within the United States at (800) 762-2974, outside the United States at (317) 572-3993 or fax (317) 572-4002.

Wiley also publishes its books in a variety of electronic formats. Some content that appears in print may not be available in electronic formats. For more information about Wiley products, visit our web site at www.wiley.com.

Library of Congress Cataloging-in-Publication Data is Available:

ISBN: 9781119840763 (cloth)
ISBN: 9781119840787 (ePub)
ISBN: 9781119840794 (ePDF)

Cover design: Paul McCarthy

SKY10040921_010523

FOR THOSE WHO RAISED ME, MUM AND ERIKA
FOR THOSE WHO SHAPED ME, TREVOR, CHRIS, AND BORAY
FOR THOSE WHO MADE ME, MAI-LAN, EDEN, AND ANAÏS

CONTENTS

Contents

ACKNOWLEDGMENTS

THANK YOU, MAI-LAN, FOR YOUR enduring love and belief.

Thank you, Eden and Anaïs, for your constant inspiration.

Thank you, Mum and Erika, for recounting some difficult but also loving memories.

To Jessie and Shannon at Wiley, thank you for seeing my potential.

To Julie, for persevering through my first draft.

To Debbie, for the quality control.

To Justin, Darren, Rachel, Dawid, Anji, Bola, Maria, Marisa, and Natalie at #Talkaboutblack, for keeping me going.

To the Diversity Project, for providing #Talkaboutblack with a platform to make a difference.

To Andrien, for always challenging the status quo and taking on the school program.

To my unofficial editors for the unabashed feedback, Trevor, Chris, Boray, Nick, Bob, Tilly Justin, Darren, Keith, Arlene, Professor Keith and Tiffany.

To the authors of the Black Wealth Creation Report, Marcel, Fayemi, Naomi, and Princella.

To the Inequality Risk project group, Jovan, David, David, Chris, Daniela, and Tim.

INTRODUCTION

THE CITY OF LONDON IS the UK's financial district. It's often referred to as the Square Mile because it covers an area roughly 1.12 square miles or 2.90km^2.[1] Glass-covered modern buildings are occupied by banks, asset managers, accountants, insurers, and lawyers, cogs in a machine that generates approximately 22% of the UK's GDP.[2] Among these new buildings are churches, sculptures, and plaques, which signpost the City of London's rich history, but it's incredibly easy to miss them. Busy executives rush from one meeting to another, and on the odd occasion they have some respite from the demands of corporate life, their attention is consumed by mobile phones, even as the hideous figures known as Grotesques on Gracechurch Street gaze down upon them.[3] There is one sculpture which, ashamedly, I must have walked past a dozen times before I paid it any heed. On September 4, 2008, Archbishop Desmond Tutu unveiled a monument that commemorates the abolition of the transatlantic slave trade in 1807. The artwork consists of a group of granite columns protruding out of the ground. Entitled *Gilt of Cain*, it is a collaboration between sculptor Michael Visocchi and poet Lemn Sissay.[4] Extracts from Sissay's poem "Gilt of Cain" are engraved into the stone.

> *Cash flow runs deep but spirit deeper*
> *You ask Am I my brothers keeper?*
> *I answer by nature by spirit by rightful laws*
> *My name, my brother, Wilberforce.*

It's tempting to focus on the fact that the poem and sculpture address the abolition of slavery, particularly given the reference to William Wilberforce (August 24, 1759–July 29, 1833). Wilberforce was a British politician, philanthropist, and leader of the movement to end the slave trade.[5] But Sissay's poem is also littered with references to the economics of this period:

> *The dealer lied when the dealer said*
> *the bull was charging the bear was dead,*
> *the market must calculate per capita, not head.*
> *And great traders acting in concert, arms rise*
> *as the actuals frought on the sea of franchise*
> *thrown overboard into the exchange to drown*
> *in distressed brokers disconsolate frown.*
> *In Accounting liquidity is a mounting morbidity*
> *but raising the arms with such rigid rapidity . . .*

The sculptures jutting out of the ground are shaped in the form of sugar cane, a staple and valuable commodity during the slave era, and adorned with excerpts from Sissay's poem.

Similarly, I have now lost count of the number of times I have visited New York, either for business or pleasure, and knew nothing of the slave market that once occupied Wall Street. Wall Street itself was an actual wall, erected by the Dutch to keep out Native Americans who might attack the area.[6] But between 1711 and 1762, on the corner of Wall Street and Pearl Street, there was an active market where enslaved were traded.[7] On June 27, 2015, Mayor Bill DeBlasio dedicated a plaque commemorating the site in Lower Manhattan.[8]

I never really questioned my "right" to establish a career in finance. Often being the only Black person in the room, I always felt like an outsider, a guest, on tenterhooks in the event that my pass ran out and I would be asked to leave. Yet, as a British person of Caribbean heritage, my very being is inextricably linked with this world. Black people helped create the wealth of the US, the UK, and Europe, yet we don't participate in it. I do, however, recognize the difference that working in finance has made to my life after growing up in a single-parent family in inner-city London where, on paper at least, my life chances were poor. The journey has been difficult and there are still too few who are able to even conceive of embarking on anything similar. This is a waste—of potential, of life, and of opportunity. So the question is, what can I do to equip others with the belief to take the first step and how can I change the world to accept them?

The Black diaspora is not monolithic, but many segments of the Black community in today's Western democracies face a range of challenges, including higher rates of unemployment, poorer physical and mental health, lower educational attainment, and higher rates of imprisonment or incarceration than our White counterparts. When we think about these challenges, we tend to see these as a social construct caused by the way someone treats us, interacts with us, or behaves toward us. I am 44 years old, live a pretty middle-class life-style, and yet when I'm heading back from the gym wearing a tracksuit and I pop into the supermarket, I may still find myself being followed by a security guard. This is demeaning, and the cumulative effects of this cause significant physical and emotional harm. However, my life outcomes cannot be solely attributed to situations like this. Social advantage must be created alongside economic advantage. For example, the prevention of discrimination of Black patients must come alongside equal access to healthcare; preventing the school-teacher from negatively stereotyping Black pupils must come alongside the opportunity to receive a quality educa-tion; and equality of opportunity through promotion in the business world must come alongside equal pay. This book will argue that the key challenges Black communities face stem from our economic position and that the way to over-come them is to change our economic situation alongside combating social prejudice. This "socioeconomic inequality" needs to be deconstructed, because to date the economic considerations have been neglected.

To fully understand this economic inequality, we must assess the origins. We find that they are rooted in the histories of Western democracies through the transatlantic slave trade, industrialization, and the growth of capitalism. These pivotal periods changed both the economic fortunes of the United States and Europe, with vast amounts of wealth created, but concentrated in the hands of a few segments of society. This wealth—which we define as the economic value of assets such as property, land, business interests, and income—affords access to healthcare, education, and employment and improves the life outcomes of individuals. Meanwhile, this same period saw African states and the descendants of the 10 million enslaved who were transported across the Atlantic

Ocean and who now reside in the Americas, the Caribbean, and Europe systematically prevented from accumulating wealth, which has had a detrimental impact on their life outcomes.[9]

Today, the legacy of this period is plain to see. Our finance system, from banking to insurance or broking, was built during this period and shaped the dominant economic belief system of Western capitalism. Meanwhile, our education, policing, judicial, and health systems have been created to operate in this system.

Attempts to improve the life outcomes of Black communities have been both piecemeal and focused on the symptoms of economic inequality rather than the causes. This might be the crime rates experienced in the Black community being met with increasingly forceful methods of policing and imprisonment or incarceration rather than understanding that they are more likely to be victims of crime and that the issue is one rooted in social deprivation due to the economic position and lack of economic opportunities Black communities face. When we have seen attempts to reduce the racial wealth gap, they have tended to focus on one segment of an individual's life, rather than across an individual's life journey. So if we are to reduce the wealth gap, it can't only be focused on educational attainment; we also need to understand the household a child is born into, their access to healthcare, their ability to enter the workplace, their capacity to be paid and promoted equally, and their adequate retirement and healthcare provisions. By creating an "index," it can allow us to set a benchmark for progression of different cohorts and make and measure interventions during an individual's life.

One might argue that creating economic freedom in a system constructed on racial inequality is impossible, that the system itself requires wholesale change. Others are concerned the progression of Black communities means the regression of White communities, often referred to as a zero-sum game. If we are spending a significant portion of a county's gross domestic product on policing, healthcare, and our prison systems, this presents an ongoing economic burden on a country. And yet there is no universal measure for this risk, and consequently it goes unnoticed. This is in stark contrast to other risks such as inflation, interest rates, longevity, and increasingly climate, geopolitical conflicts, and a pandemic, which are all measured. If we can develop a measure for inequality, it can be monitored and mitigated by governments and corporations. Measuring racial inequality risk presents the prospect of measuring gender, class, or even geographical risks—risks that also impact White communities. The creation of risk measures for Black economic inequality could be transformative for all. These risks are measured and mitigated not because of an individual's belief or values, but because they make rational economic sense.[10]

Furthermore, the creation of an index alongside an understanding of its economic impact presents us with an opportunity to gain social and economic value from Black communities. This may mean bringing more people who have a host of attributes into firms in this era of social, political, and economic upheaval. It might mean releasing their economic potential by increasing productivity. Or it may mean contributing to economic output by tapping into Black consumerism. The following chapters detail my own experience of much of the above, from a council estate in London to the senior levels of finance.

Some names and places have been changed to protect identities.

PROLOGUE

WHEN ADDRESSING THE CHALLENGES THAT segments of the Black community in today's Western democracies face, the discussion typically focuses on poor mental and physical health outcomes, lower educational attainment, higher rates of unemployment, and greater rates of imprisonment or incarceration than our White counterparts. The discussion also tends to focus on social interactions or behaviors directed toward Black people as the cause of these challenges. For example, poor educational attainment among Black children is often seen as a result of a schoolteacher's bias or higher rates or imprisonment due to prejudices in the judicial system. These undoubtedly have an impact on the ability of Black communities to progress, and we should continue to combat this. However, the removal of these alone are not enough to change the life outcomes of Black communities. By comparison, White communities in Western democracies experience better life outcomes and much of this is due to their ability to access healthcare, education, and maximize opportunities in the workplace. Any attempt to improve the life outcomes of Black communities, whether in the realm of better physical and mental health, better performance in education, or progression in the workplace or business world, needs to tackle the economic factors. Instead, to date, we focus on the symptoms of inequality rather than the cause.

To truly change our position in society requires access to adequate healthcare alongside fair and unbiased patient treatment; it requires access to quality education alongside unbiased teaching practices; and it requires equality of opportunity in the business world, whether employment, progression, or equal pay alongside fair treatment by line managers. These challenges are economic in nature and it is the combination of these two elements, both the social and economic challenges, that comprise "socioeconomic inequality." But while a significant portion of time has been spent understanding the societal factors, less has been spent analyzing the economic considerations. Increasing the economic opportunity of the Black community so it is at least comparable to our White counterparts, what we typically refer to as the reducing the wealth gap, is critical to improving this community's life outcomes.

Attempts to increase the economic position of Black people today have so far been piecemeal rather than understanding that the deprivation is compounded over the course of an individual's life. So if we are to truly tackle this, we need to find a method of tracking the life journey of an individual, what advantages or disadvantages they might have, and what interventions are necessary. For example, what are the prospects for a Black girl born in a single-parent family on a lower income when compared to a White boy born with both parents present, in a higher-income household. If we can track this, we might be able to assess what interventions can make a difference to the Black girl's life. This may also allow us to assess the economic contribution of different groups within society and not only measure the risk of not improving their life outcomes but also the contribution to a country's economy. If we can treat inequality risk in the similar way to other risks—interest rates, inflation, and longevity, but also climate, geopolitical, and now pandemic risk—it moves this discussion from being one of values and beliefs to one of rational decision-making. Furthermore, applying this successfully to reduction of racial inequality opens the possibility of reducing other inequalities such as gender or class, inequalities that impact a cross-section of diasporas.

However, if we are to dismantle the wealth gap, we need to understand its origins and how it manifests today. Our finance system, from banking and insurance to broking and wealth management, influences Western democracies' political systems and social stratification. After all, our education, policing, judicial, and healthcare systems have been designed to operate within this construct. To begin to unravel this complex and interwoven societal system, we must start with the birth of capitalism and the transatlantic slave trade.

This is my story, but we all have a part to play. I can see the opportunity; I hope you will too.

1

Onion

THE FIRST TIME I SAW the Royal Exchange, in London's financial district, was during a bus ride when I was about 18 years old. Music was a big part of my life, and I would travel across London to independent record shops with one of my closest friends, Jamie, to search for obscure hip-hop records, often costing a fortune because they were imported from the United States. This particular day we were sitting at the back of the bus, traveling back from East London to North London. I began to notice the increasingly grandiose buildings that seemed to sprout from the ground and stretch high into the sky. When the bus turned a corner, I was taken aback by the sight of what seemed like hundreds of people in suits teeming out of buildings, presumably on their way to buy lunch or rushing to an important business meeting. My first reaction was one of awe: this seemed like a different world. I grew up in the inner city in what was then a poor, predominately Black neighborhood. I had no concept of the world of finance, so much so that I wasn't actually sure what I was looking at. My second reaction was one of inspiration: I was studying and had achieved very good grades at school, and depending on the outcome of my final exams there was the possibility that I would gain acceptance to one of the UK's top universities. I had no idea what career I would forge but knew this seemed like a place I should be.

The second time I saw the Royal Exchange was after I graduated, on my way to an interview for an investment bank based in Bishopsgate. This was before the age of smartphones and GPS, so to find my way I printed a map and memorized the route. "Exit 7 at Bank tube station, walk past the Bank of England and onto Cornhill and then turn left onto Bishopsgate," Easy—except I wrongly assumed the Royal Exchange was the Bank of England, as many people still do today. Given its importance, the Bank of England is surprisingly nondescript. And so I got completely lost and ended up somewhere near Aldgate, which is a good 20 minutes away from the Royal Exchange. Asking for directions was fruitless; it was impossible to get the attention of the stream of people as they walked past, their pace spinning me on my heels. I eventually asked a Black cab driver for directions, but that wasn't before two others drove off just before I got close enough to ask. He directed me back toward Bishopsgate, where I walked past the Royal Exchange once again before finding the right building with about five minutes to spare.

"Can I help you, sir?" A security guard stopped me as I entered the revolving doors. "I'm here for an interview," I replied. "May I see some ID?" he asked. I pulled the letter of confirmation out of my bag and showed it to the grey-haired guard. He scrutinized it and then said, "Right, over to the reception desk." The lady behind the desk greeted me with a smile and asked me to sit with some other eager interviewees. I sat and gazed around the huge lobby. Some people were clearly regulars, saying hello to the security guard as they entered. Some were visitors; however, the security guard did not stop any of them.

"So you have good qualifications, and we really like the way you handled the case study we gave you. But one thing we're interested in is why you only worked at a supermarket whilst you were at university. Some of our other applicants have traveled, built schools in Africa. They're incredibly well-rounded. Do you feel you have as much to offer?" I have gone back in time and answered this question too many times. The archetype for a finance professional is easy to define. They've often attended the same universities, studied the same degree, and have pursued the same extracurricular activities. They're typically high-performing and function well with clear parameters. But the world is changing and when faced with a challenge for which there is no rule book, I've seen many flounder. Too much emphasis is placed upon ticking these boxes rather than attributes. I wish I had told the interviewer I couldn't afford to quit my job because it was a lifeline that enabled me to attend university. The risk of giving this up to go somewhere during the summer felt too great to bear. And at the same time, I paid my own way through university and sacrificed a lot. It was only when I eventually reached a senior position and embraced my journey that it became a virtue rather than something to shy away from. But at the time, comparing myself to candidates who had built schools in Africa felt futile.

As I left the building I walked back out through the revolving doors and made the fatal mistake of not seeing a sign that said DO NOT PUSH. The door stopped abruptly, briefly trapping me and a dark-suited gentleman in the door opposite. I couldn't hear what he was saying but from the look on his face he was angry, spit flying from his mouth as he admonished me. I walked back toward Bank tube station and past the Royal Exchange for the fourth time.

Trying to understand your place in the world is similar to peeling an onion: you remove one layer only to find another. The Royal Exchange was created by Sir Thomas Gresham in 1566 and was designed to be London's first exchange dedicated to trading goods, services, and stocks.[1] It was officially opened in 1571 by Queen Elizabeth I, who gave the exchange its royal title and a licence to sell alcohol. Today the Royal Exchange still houses luxury goods and is a great place to grab a coffee on a discreet upper floor, which is a favorite haunt of the city's headhunters priming candidates to make a big money move.[2] To enter the building, you walk up an imposing set of stairs and through eight large columns. Above this are sculptures of a number of figures, which can be easily missed unless you take the time to look. I worked in the city for 20 years before someone pointed out the scene. These figures represent Britain's global trading activities in the 16th century. The dominant figure stares fixedly across the City with a crown upon her head. You'd be forgiven for mistaking this central figure for a religious or even royal figure. But it actually represents Commerce, holding a "charter of exchange in one hand" and a ship's rudder in the other. Alongside Commerce, other figures include a Turkish merchant doing his accounts, an Armenian banker, and a Chinese man trading opium. But to the left is another man, the only figure who is not standing or trading, but kneeling: an African man dressed in only a loincloth in a display of subservience at the table of commerce.[3]

The kneeling man is still there today, and he serves as a reminder, a bookmark if you will, of the origins of the socio-economic position of Black communities.

The first layer of the onion I peeled back was the realization that this period shaped not just our social standing but also our familial structures. When I was at school there was never any discussion about this era of British history. We did study the British industrial revolution, but not the preceding era, which contributed to it. I also knew my family was from Jamaica but never understood how and why my family arrived there. I even studied history at university and took electives in African history, but shied away from the slavery modules because I thought I knew all I needed to about this period.

The triangular slave trade commenced around 1500 and concluded in the 1865. European nations forcibly removed millions of people from West and Central Africa and shipped them, in horrific conditions, across the Atlantic. The trade was considered "triangular" because traders set out from European ports and headed to Africa's west coast. From there they bought people in exchange for goods and placed them chained and shackled into ships. The voyage across the Atlantic, the "Middle Passage," took six to eight weeks to complete and those who were fortunate enough to survive the journey were sold off and enslaved to new owners. The ships then returned to Europe with goods produced by the enslaved such as sugar, coffee, or cotton. From there the ships would set off again to return to Africa. What more did I need to know? That is, until my aunt, who had traced my family history, told me about the gaping hole in my family's lineage.

My grandmother Winifred Agatha Lewis, nee Stewart, was born in 1926 in Spanish Town, Jamaica. To me, "Spanish Town" was just a name; I never made any connection to this and the history of the island, yet it was a clue to Jamaica's past.

The island of Xaymaca, which was later dubbed Jamaica by the Spanish, was located in an archipelago between North and South America. It was originally inhabited by the Redware people, called such because of the red earth artefacts they left on the island.[4] But it was the Arawakan Taino people with light brown skin and coarse hair who dominated the island. They arrived on the island after the Redware people and relied on subsistence farming and fishing. They traveled to the island from South America and built small settlements inland by the shore.[5] The Taino lived a peaceful existence until 1494 and the arrival of Christopher Columbus, who had set out to discover the East Indies but instead came across what he eventually termed the West Indies. Columbus originally arrived at St. Ann's Bay to the north of the island but was attacked by the Taino, who didn't recognize the strange-looking guests. Columbus then sailed further down the coast to Discovery Bay, docked, and went on the offensive, overwhelming the Taino and declaring ownership of the island on behalf of Spain. The Spanish then set about killing and torturing any Taino who resisted. Others were forced to work on establishing Spanish settlements. Many died from the conditions they were forced to work in, and the remaining Taino perished after coming into contact with European diseases from which they had no immunity. The island only really served as an outpost for refueling and replenishing supplies to Spanish ships and remained poor as a result. Most of the settlements remained insignificant, with the exception of St. Jago de la Vega, or "Spanish Town," which eventually became the capital. The Spanish required labor initially for agricultural production and the mining of gold and silver in Peru and Mexico.[6]

My grandfather Tivy St Ledger was born in 1905. His nickname at school was Brass Head Jimmy because his hair had a reddish tint. He worked as a boiler man for the national gas company, which was considered a very good job. His mother, my great-grandmother, was called Catherine Emily McClymont, aka Miss Katie. She spoke "proper" English, which at the time was unusual for someone who lived in the countryside. When I read about my family history, there is a touch of pride. The Lewises were considered cultured because they sat at a dining table for dinner and food was served in separate dishes rather than from the pot. The silver was always polished and Tivy would ring a bell for dinner. My aunt was able to trace my family history right back to my great-great-great-grandfathers but then the history stops.

Slave ships kept little record of their cargo, and in any case it may have been futile. Not only was the name Lewis bestowed upon my family after the slave owners themselves, but there was also a breakdown of the Black family structure during this period. The community I grew up in had a mixture of family structures, from nuclear family to single-parent households, which included my own. At the time this seemed normal because I really had nothing to compare my experience to. But reflecting on this now, I'm struck by the number of single mothers raising their children. I certainly became aware of my own absent father, an awareness that increased as I grew older. I'm struck by the ability of the Black family to survive slavery but can't help but ask whether the disruption of the Black family now has its roots in the dissolution of the Black family then. Upon enslavement, men, women, and children were separated before being transported; this not only broke the family structure but also cultural practices. Once Black people arrived at their destination there was still no guarantee of stability. Black people who were enslaved often did have relationships and families; a large number of the enslaved grew up with both parents and often grandparents. But there was always the threat that these family units would also be broken up. In her autobiography *Incidents in the Life of a Slave Girl,* formerly enslaved Harriet Jacobs describes a mother being parted from her seven children.

> *On one of these sale days, I saw a mother lead seven children to the auction-block. She knew that some of them would be taken from her; but they took all. The children were sold to a slave-trader, and their mother was bought by a man in her own town. Before night her children were all far away. She begged the trader to tell her where he intended to take them; this he refused to do. How could he, when he knew he would sell them, one by one, wherever he could command the highest price? I met that mother in the street, and her wild, haggard face lives to-day in my mind. She wrung her hands in anguish, and exclaimed, "Gone! All gone! Why don't God kill me?" I had no words wherewith to comfort her. Instances of this kind are of daily, yea, of hourly occurrence.[7]*

Another layer of the onion I peeled is that this period also saw the origins of the economic position of Black communities. There are often discussions about why so much attention should be given to the Transatlantic Slave Trade, after all slavery has existed throughout human history. Should the British still be upset with the Italians for the Roman Empire? The Transatlantic Slave Trade was different, however. Not only did it prepare America and Britain for their industrial revolutions, but it actually laid the foundations for the creation of capitalism, the system that today governs not only our institutions, but also our social order and even values. The socioeconomic position of Black communities which we still see today is a direct result of this era.

It could be argued that the European nations' conquests of Africa were primarily driven by views about race and White superiority and this debate has rumbled for years. In 1968, historian Winthrop D. Jordan published a study of racial stereotypes, *White Over Black: American Attitudes Toward the Negro 1550–1812*. He identified three related perspectives, which justified the enslavement of Africans due to purely social considerations. The first is the association of the color Black with all things dirty, filthy, or unclean. When Jordan published his study, the *Oxford English Dictionary* defined black as "deeply stained with dirt; soiled, dirty, foul." Secondly, due to the differences in the customs and behavior of Africans, they were seen as uncivilized and savages and finally as heathen and un-Christian. Given this view that Africans were barely human, enslavement of Black people was a natural evolution of the concept of White superiority. By contrast, Eric Williams in *Capitalism & Slavery* (1944) and more recent authors such David Eltis in *The Rise of African Slavery in the Americas* (2000) contend that racism was an economic consequence of slavery. In the 17th and 18th centuries, poor White and African Black people were enslaved, but the abundance of Africans meant they became the product of choice. The reality is that both social beliefs were utilized to justify the economic imperative; these beliefs about Africans conveniently created a narrative, which was fueled by the export of 3.1 million enslaved Africans between 1640 and 1807 to the Caribbean, North and South America, and other British colonies.[8] The enslaved Africans were a source of labor that provided a workforce able to turn raw materials such as sugar cane into tradable goods such as refined sugar. Typically, a company pays workers a wage, which is deducted from profits, but African slaves were seen as "chattel," property to be owned and traded at will once bought—in other words, free labor.

Once we understand the motivations, we the need to examine why these social and economic disadvantages still exist today. The purpose of capitalism is to generate profit, and although capitalism at this time was embryonic, the transatlantic slave trade was very lucrative.

The trade was initially led by the Spanish and Portuguese. From 1441 they began to enslave Africans but were only exporting them after the discovery of the Americas presented the opportunity to further their economic interests.[9] Other European nations soon saw the opportunity. The Dutch colonized several West African states and the territories in the Caribbean such as Curaçao. The French seized several African states and colonized islands such as Martinique.[10] Britain colonized Barbados, Maryland, and Virginia and, in 1618 King James I gave a charter of monopoly to 30 London merchants to engage in the enslavement and trafficking of Africans.[11] Britain dabbled in an array of goods and products and through its colonies in the Caribbean became the world's leading supplier of sugar. By the 1800s economic activity related to slavery, including exports, plantation production, and the industries that depended on the plantation complex, comprised 10 to 12% of the country's gross domestic product (GDP). This is significant when we consider that at this time, Britain operated a predominately agrarian economy.[12] By the 1760s annual exports from the Caribbean alone to Britain were worth over £3 million, which is the equivalent of £250 million today.[13]

This period also saw the creation of hugely profitable joint-stock entities such as the Royal Africa Company and the East India Company, which covered outgoings such as shipping costs but also allowed the trade in slavery to be conducted at scale. In the 17th century, the Royal Africa Company could buy an enslaved African with trade goods worth £3 but then have that person sold in the Americas for £20. The average profit of the Royal Africa Company in the in the 1680s was 38% per voyage.[14]

And then there was the advent of practices such as insurance. Given the outlay, trading companies and independent traders protected themselves against any losses, usually through disease or mutiny during the Middle Passage. It's tempting to see many of these institutions as archaic and of a different era, but many are still preeminent today; the original founders changed their social standing and became rich. The wealth gap is as much about those who have amassed a fortune as those who were denied. In the UK, the University College London undertook a project called *Legacies of British Slave Ownership,* which revealed that 10 to 20% of Britain's wealthy can be identified as having a significant link to slavery.[15]

If the Caribbean were synonymous with the production of sugar, the American South became intrinsically linked with the production of cotton. In 1789, there were less than half a million slaves in the American South, but by 1860 this had ballooned to almost four million.[16] Before cotton, expensive linen was used to clothe people; cotton offered a much more durable and cost-effective alternative. The demand was such that the slave owners in the South became the country's first millionaires. Cotton had to be processed and milled and this became the chief focus of the textile manufacturers in New England. Boston and New York were dominated by merchants who traded cotton and other goods produced by the enslaved.

A further layer of the onion is that this period also shaped culture and even how to exist day-to-day within financial institutions and corporations. Finance is known for its social aspects, to relieve pressure for a challenging day at the office but also to develop relationships with colleagues and clients. This was certainly one of the more difficult adjustments I had to make during my career in the city because much of this revolved around common areas of interest and the consumption of alcohol. In the UK, this often takes the form of discussions about rugby, a very middle-class sport, which I had little knowledge of. Add to that the fact that I don't drink a lot. Your ability to connect with others in this manner often determines whether you land a deal or a promotion, and for many corporations it was the culture. If we wish to make contact with someone today, we can simply pick up the phone, drop them a message, or arrange a video conference. To exchange goods and services, we now have a complex system of banks and exchanges underpinned by robust legal systems and the ability to complete exchanges electronically. But before this infrastructure was established, coffeehouses were the place to exchange goods and develop relationships. Coffeehouses were small establishments where you went to meet a particular type of merchant and their continued existence is one of the enduring features of the preindustrial period.

A favorite haunt in the City of London is the Jampot, a pub hidden behind in a small alleyway off Cornhill. The actual name of the establishment is the Jamaica Wine House. When I first visited the pub it felt like a novelty, a pub named after the island where my mother was born. Of course, then I walked in and there were no Black people, just grey-haired white men, a few women, and, well, me. I assumed the name was simply made up by the owners rather than being a landmark for the history of capitalism.

In the 18th century familial ties were critical; your network was everything. For example, if you were in the insurance or shipping business you would probably frequent William Lloyd's Coffee House in London because it was the first place to receive maritime news. This was the place to congregate to arrange insurance but also to buy and sell the enslaved. It was the precursor of Lloyds of London, the marketplace for insurance, which still exists today.[17] If you had an interest in goods from the Caribbean, such as sugar produced in Barbados or Jamaica, you would visit the Jamaica Coffee House. This fact is not hidden; outside the Jampot there is a blue plaque that reads, "Here stood the first London Coffee House at the sign of the Pasqua Rose Head 1652." Pasqua Rose was a Dalmatian who established the premises after importing coffee from Jamaica as well as goods from Turkey.[18] It is somewhat bemusing how important this site is but even the Jampot's website makes little reference to the role the establishment played in the slave trade or its role in creating the City of London; rather there are some quizzical comments over the references to Jamaica. "They only serve one type of rum," says one review. Another states its importance is due to Samuel Pepys, a notable naval administrator famed for his diaries, which give us a unique insight into the period. Pepys visited the coffeehouse in 1660,[19] despite the fact that he became a shareholder in the Royal Adventurers in Africa in 1663 and owned enslaved Africans himself. Another entry from Pepys diary discusses him being entertained by the banker Sir Robert Vyner, who showed him "a black boy that he had that had died of consumption." Vyner dried the boy in an oven and then placed him in a box to be displayed to visitors.[20] The economic considerations are important, but this is a vivid example of how much disregard there was for Black lives.

The influence of this period even impacts our language. The world of finance is littered with acronyms and technical terms; people who work outside of the industry hearing two finance professionals talk must think it sounds like a different language. Even with my 20 years' experience there is still a host of terms I've never heard before. During a meeting with a prospective client, the discussion turned to new investment ideas and the benefits of a tontine. I had never heard the term before, so I listened intently to the discussion and as soon as I left the meeting, I did some research. A tontine is a retirement investment approach whereby investors pay into a plan and upon the death of an individual, proceeds are shared amongst the remaining investors. It wasn't until I dug a little deeper and peeled another layer from the onion that I found out that one of the largest tontines in the United States was established during the slave era.

Tontines were named after Lorenzo de Tonti, a 17th-century Italian banker who modified a similar approach created by a Belgian Nicolas Bourey, and they were often utilized by national governments or kings to raise money to finance wars.[21] In 1792, 24 US stockbrokers signed an agreement that attempted to cut out the middlemen and stated that the brokers would only trade with one another. Legend has it that this was signed under a buttonwood tree, and it became known as the Buttonwood Agreement.[22] This became the founding document of the New York Stock Exchange, a pivotal agreement in the history of US financial history. To conduct business the brokers needed a venue, and the Tontine Coffee House was created. Also demonstrating the link between social aspects and economic was the fact that this was located at 82 Wall Street and was established in 1794 as a tontine with the construction being financed by the selling of 203 shares.[23] Each share was valued at $200, which gave the Tontine Coffee House start-up capital of $40,000, the equivalent of $1 million today.[24] The Tontine Coffee House became a hub for traders with goods such as cotton, sugar, and the enslaved. This also spurred the same industry as in Britain with shipping, insurance, and financing, scaling the exportation to the extent that by the eve of the American Civil War, America went from being a marginal player in the global economy to raw cotton accounting for 61% of the value of all US products shipped abroad.[25] The coffeehouse eventually wound down in 1817 as the brokers launched a new venue at 40 Wall Street, the New York Stock Exchange, the world's largest exchange, which had a market capitalisation of $27.7 trillion as of May 5, 2022, highlighting just how much wealth the slave era helped create.[26]

But perhaps the most important consequence of this period is that it crystallized the social and economic status of the enslaved following the abolition of slavery. In his seminal work *The Wealth of Nations,* published in 1776, Adam Smith put forward the idea of free market conomics.[27] This classical view of economics originated in France through Jean-Baptiste Colbert, comptroller of finance, who under King Louis XIV asked industrialists what the government could do to help businesses and was told "leave us alone." This approach of *laissez-faire* was therefore based on minimal government intervention in the economic affairs of individuals and society. This encompassed many of the structures that had arisen through slavery such as a division of labor, which increases productivity through specialization of tasks, and prices being established by market forces rather than being centrally controlled.

Slavery was problematic for Smith's theory because he believed that left to their own devices, individuals would maximize their own economic output and create wealth for themselves and society. However, someone who was enslaved was not motivated because there was no reward, so this was inefficient. Freeing the enslaved would therefore create a more productive society, but only if they were given the means to participate. Property ownership in particular is important in a functioning capitalist system because the owner is incentivized to work hard to increase its value. For example, if you own your property and the price of your house increases, you are entitled to that increase in value. This then provides the owner with the means to sell or rent their house and increase their wealth. A further requirement to participate in capitalism is access to education. This encompasses basic reading and writing skills; vocational training, which allows the individual to enter a specialist field (such as carpentry or engineering); but also the aspiration to maximize one's own wealth in the capitalist system. A laissez-faire approach works, but not if you have no property, skills, or capital; instead, it can have the opposite effect and increase inequality, which in itself is inefficient, something my solutions will attempt to rectify.

Slavery was outlawed in Great Britain in 1807 and abolished in 1833, and June 19, 1865—"Juneteenth"—in the United States. This was two and a half years after President Abraham Lincoln ordered those who were enslaved to gain their independence through the Emancipation Proclamation and two months after the Confederate army surrendered, ending the US Civil War. As the Civil War battles fizzled out, leaders of the Union gathered together a group of Black ministers in Savannah, Georgia, with the intent to initially help 40,000 of the 4 million former enslaved. Out of this meeting came General William T. Sherman's Special Field Order 15, which aimed to provide lands along the southeast coast so that "each family shall have a plot of not more than forty acres of tillable ground." This order become known as 40 acres and a mule. In a decision that still has repercussions today, President Andrew Johnson, who was a former owner of enslaved Africans himself and a staunch advocate of White supremacy, overturned the decision by the end of 1865 and returned the land to the slave owners who had originally owned it. Black people in the United States, as well as the Caribbean and South America, were denied one of the critical tenants to participate in the capitalist system: land and property ownership. To get some sense of the economic impact, the value of the 40 acres for the 40,000 enslaved who were denied ownership would be $640 billion today.[28]

These are the origins of the social and economic disadvantages of today's Black communities. I had to get to the center of the onion to begin to understand why Black people are still kneeling.

2

Six Hours

SUNDAYS WERE A SPECIAL DAY in my house. I remember vividly the prospect of eating dinner, which was a traditional Caribbean affair of fried chicken and rice and peas. My mum would soak the peas overnight before adding long-grain American rice, which she would buy from the local supermarket. The smell wafted through our council flat, which meant salivating all day before finally eating at around 6 p.m. Sunday was also the day my mum washed, combed, and plaited my sister's hair. This was an all-day event, with the smell of fried chicken growing stronger against the whirring of the hair dryer. Black women's hair is often a defining characteristic, and it takes a lot of care. My sister had to wake up at least 30 minutes earlier to grease and style her hair before going to work. Sundays were often preceded by a visit to the shops to buy hair products.

We lived in a neighborhood called Tottenham, which at the time was heavily populated by a Caribbean com-|munity. Gentrification and migration trends have seen this community decline over the years, but such was the presence of Jamaicans, Barbadians, and St. Lucians that the high street had an array of Caribbean hairdressers and barber shops, the largest being a 20-minute bus ride away. This shop attracted Caribbean and West African shoppers alike, with every conceivable product for sale; hair weaves, hair clippers, cocoa butter, you name it, you'd find it there. There was one other distinguishing characteristic, however: the shop wasn't owned by Caribbeans or West Africans but by a Pakistani company. Even as a young child I was struck by this. Credit must be given to the owners who spotted and filled a gap in the market, but I did wonder why, as a Black community, we rarely owned our own businesses or why we wouldn't sell our own products to each other.

Today my neighbors are of Indian heritage, and they recently renovated their house. We were thinking of making some changes to our place, so we asked them for the details of their builders. They were Indian and their architect was Indian too. In fact, everyone from the suppliers to the painters and decorators were Indian. When I tried to apply the same approach to the renovation of our house, I could identify a Black builder, who happened to be my best friend, and I managed to find a Black surveyor, but after that I was stumped. There are actually many successful Black businesses, but there does seem to be lack of connectivity, and quite simply we don't have enough of them.

This then set me off on search to find the equivalent. Maybe this was a UK phenomenon. After all, the Black community is smaller here. Maybe it is different in the United States. I thought maybe this needed to be an economic study, but fortuitously one of my favorite rappers, Killer Mike — one half of the duo Run the Jewels — recorded a Netflix documentary in which he attempted to survive for three days by only buying goods and services provided by Black people and businesses in Atlanta. Atlanta has long held a reputation for being a center of Black wealth and economic prosperity. If there is any place in the Western world where a Black economic ecosystem exists, it would seem to be here. However, Killer Mike's mission proved to be impossible. In one scene, he has to sleep on a park bench because there was no Black-owned hotel, and his disappointment is palpable when he finally finds a place to eat, only to have to stop eating when the other half of Run the Jewels, El-P, points out to Mike that the food he is eating was not sourced through a Black business. The true picture is even more stark: according to the NAACP, the US dollar circulates for 28 days in Asian communities and 19 days in Jewish communities before leaving. In the Black community? Six hours.[1]

It wasn't always this way. In 1906, a wealthy Black man from Arkansas, O.W, Gurley, moved to Tulsa, Oklahoma, and purchased over 40 acres of land. Tulsa was deeply segregated at the time but benefited from an influx of Black people who had fled from the even more oppressive Mississippi. Land ownership was critical at this time because the economy of Oklahoma was largely driven by agriculture. Ownership of land, therefore, became critical for investment and consumption and being able to participate in the mainstream economy. Gurley sold his land only to other Black people. This became a community in which Black families, entrepreneurs, and business owners presided over shops, banks, lending facilities, hotels, and schools. This epicenter of Black entrepreneurialism came to be known as Black Wall Street.[2] Capitalism at this juncture was adolescent, mature enough to enact change but yet to reach its full potential. The Black dollar in Tulsa circulated 36 to 100 times for an average length of 365 days before leading the community.[3]

If we are to find solutions to increase the circulation time of the Black dollar today, it's important to understand why that circulation time is reduced so dramatically compared to other groups. A solution is vital if we also subscribe to the view that economic inequality is a cause of disparities across mental and physical health, education, unemployment, and imprisonment.

One of my friends growing up was Kwame. He was popular, he was respected by all the other kids, and he always had a girlfriend. I was the opposite: a bit geeky and socially awkward. But we were both bright and good at our schoolwork, and we both had to hide this somewhat, because academic success was the anthesis of being "hard" or street smart. By the age of 13 or 14, Kwame began to drift away from school. We remained friends, but the importance of street credibility began to outweigh gaining good grades. Kwame eventually dropped out of school altogether and the last I heard was that he was in prison for burglary. As sad as it was, this doesn't stand out from many of the other experiences of the people I grew up with, but only now as I look back can I see a pattern. Kwame had two brothers, and there was food left in the fridge and breakfast cereal for them to eat in the morning, but when I went to their house, there was never anyone there. Kwame's mum was always working—he used to boast that she had three jobs.

In the UK, a recent report by the Runnymede Trust, an independent race equality think tank, revealed that Black households have only 10 pence of savings and assets for every £1 of White British wealth.[4] In the US, White families have the highest levels of wealth at $171,000, which is 10 times the wealth of a typical Black family of $17,150.[5] It's a disparity that has persisted for centuries. It's easy to see poor people as destined to end up in low-paying jobs, unemployed, or, worse, in the criminal justice system. But if Kwame's mum had to sacrifice parenting because she needed to work three jobs to pay for essential living expenses, maybe we should think about the problem differently. Rather than focusing exclusively on the symptoms of disenfranchisement, perhaps we should think about the cause as fundamentally an economic issue.

Wealth is the value of an individual's, a group's, or a community's money or assets accumulated over time, minus any debts. It is often seen as the key indicator of prosperity because, unlike income or wages, it fluctuates less and typically receives less taxation. To acquire wealth requires several key aspects. The first is ownership of tangible assets such as land, property, businesses, or stocks and bonds. In the decades after the American Civil War, the formerly enslaved did make some progress in securing land. For example, by 1900 Black landowners in Tunica County, Mississippi, outnumbered White landowners three to one. According to the US Department of Agriculture, there were 25,000 Black farm operators in 1910, an increase of almost 20% from 1900. Black-owned farmland in Mississippi totaled 2.2 million acres by 1910, which accounted for almost 14% of all agricultural land in the US.[6]

There were two main ways for Black people to purchase land: they could buy it from a private landowner, or they could make a claim to land offered by the federal government, such as through the Southern Homestead Act and South Carolina's Land Commission. This, however, did not result in an increase in the actual wealth of Black people, because they were prevented from maximizing the ownership opportunity before being systematically stripped of these assets. First, significantly less land was purchased than available because the former enslaved simply did not have the means to acquire the land. The size and quality of the land purchased was less than that of their White counterparts, which meant lower crop yields and a lower quality of product. Acts such as these were also seen by the Southern states as a punishment by the North. After the post–Civil

War Reconstruction period (1865–1877) and the repeal of the Southern Homestead Act in 1876, available land was sold off to large-scale purchasers. As a result, many Black farmers were subject to illegal land seizures with little grounds for legal recourse.

A second aspect of wealth acquisition is that it also needs to have the ability to be transferred (for example, through inheritance or insurance), but any wealth gained by Black people was very difficult pass on. Many Black landowners did not have legally binding wills, largely due to a mistrust of the legal system. Instead, they passed land down to their next of kin without them being a legal "heir" to the property. This meant the new landowner was unable use the land to secure loans, mortgages, or insurance. After multiple generations, the land could be owned by distant relatives who often did not know or consult with other landowners. Land was often sold off unwittingly and was susceptible to seizures through unpaid taxes, or coercion from developers who wanted to get their hands on the land.[7] Race-based life insurance began in the early 1880s and included higher rates, reduced benefits, and commission for insurance agents for policies written for Black people. When laws were passed to prevent race-based insurance rates, companies simply stopped selling insurance to Black clients.

But perhaps the most important aspect of creating wealth is the ability to acquire, grow, and pass along the intangible assets such as knowledge, skills, and aspirations. Jim Crow was originally a minstrel routine performed by Thomas Dartmouth Rice, a White man who performed the act in blackface beginning in 1828. Based upon an enslaved African who was believed to be physically disabled, the show was performed up and down the country and made "Daddy" Rice a household name.[8] The show was a precursor to the minstrel shows, which were based on racial stereotypes and were pejorative to Black people. But the term "Jim Crow" also became a set of laws used to economically disadvantage Black people after the end of slavery and of the Reconstruction period. The 1875 Civil Rights Act stated that all races have the right to equal treatment in public accommodations, housing, medical care, transport, and education.[9] However, in 1883, the US Supreme Court stated that this decision did not apply to private persons or corporations.[10]

There was some confusion about the legality of segregation until Homer Plessy boarded a train in New Orleans and sat in a car reserved for Whites only. Plessey was one-eighth Black but under the Laws of Louisiana was classified as Black. He refused to leave the carriage, and this resulted in series of court trials to assess the legality of "separate but equal." In 1892, the Supreme Court ruled this was not a violation of the Fourteenth Amendment (which granted citizenship to formerly enslaved people) and legitimized the segregation of Blacks in the American South.[11]

As a result, Black people were subject to separate and inferior schools, housing, healthcare, transportation, and churches, and thus were prevented from accessing the intangible capital that enables the acquisition of the skills, knowledge, tools, aspirations, and social cohesion required to progress. For example, many Black people from the South were attracted to the North through the belief they could participate in the region's increasing industrialization. However, although housing was not explicitly segregated along racial lines, property owners would only offer housing to Black people in areas that were predominately occupied by other Black people. These areas soon became overcrowded, and it was too difficult to access quality education and healthcare. The daily struggle prevented taking a more long-term view; to many people, for example, a focus on education seemed like a luxury. Experiences such as these also created mistrust, with Black people continuing to refuse to create a will or take advantage of hereditary rights, which would have protected what little wealth they created. This systemic prevention of economic equality of Black communities has been coupled with the systematic persecution of Black communities. It is this that creates the socioeconomic complex. To find a solution, economic progress must come alongside social advancement.

Despite the wealth accumulating on Black Wall Street (see the discussion above), on May 31, 1921, the *Tulsa Tribune* reported that a Black man, Dick Rowland, attempted to rape a White woman, Sarah Page. This was another inflection point, a period where real change could have happened. Instead, the White population in the area refused to wait for the outcome of the investigation and unleashed two days of racial violence. Thirty-five blocks were set alight, 300 people died, and 800 were injured.[12] Over 9,000 people became homeless with no reparations or recourse to compensate for their losses.[13]

There are two repercussions from this. First, it demonstrates the relationship between society and economic prosperity, commonly called social mobility. This community of Black people had utilized entrepreneurship and the capitalist system to improve their social standing. But unlike their White counterparts, who not only profited from slavery but changed their social standing, they were unable to change the social stratification that had taken hold of US society. Secondly, and perhaps most importantly, this also introduced a loss of aspiration, and of the belief that, despite limited opportunity, an entire community can progress.

A further example is that of Emmett Till. In 1955 Emmett, a 14-year-old Black teenager from Chicago, was visiting relatives in Mississippi. Emmett went to the store with his cousins and on his way out there was an interaction with the store's proprietor, Carolyn Bryant. She claimed that Emmett had grabbed her, made lewd advances, and whistled at her. This was deemed to be such an affront that Carolyn's husband, Roy Bryant, and her brother-in-law J. W. Milam kidnapped Emmett and made him carry a 75-pound cotton gin fan to the banks of the Tallahatchie River. They then ordered him to remove his clothes before beating him to near death, gouging out his eye, and finally shooting him in the head. His body was tied to the gin fan with barbed wire and dumped in the river.

Emmett's body was found three days later but it was so disfigured it could only be identified by a ring he was wearing. The authorities wanted a quick burial but Emmett's mother requested his body be flown home to Chicago and arranged an open-casket funeral so the world could see what had happened to her son. *Jet*, a Black weekly magazine, published a picture of Emmett's bloated face and the mainstream press picked up on the story. On September 23, 1955, after less than an hour of deliberating, an all-White jury returned a verdict of not guilty of murder or kidnapping because they believed the state had failed to prove the identity of the body. Bryant and Milam would later confess to the killing but due to the double-jeopardy provision of the law, they could not be tried twice. Even the outrage many people felt failed to overturn the decision.[14] Tim Tyson, author of the book *The Blood of Emmett Till* (2017), detailed that during an interview with Carolyn, she confessed that Emmett never touched or harassed her, saying, "Nothing that boy did could ever justify what happened to him."

The murder of Emmett Till unleashed a chain of events that threatened to change the racial landscape of America. That same year, on December 1, 42-year-old Rosa Parks was commuting home by bus after working all day at the Montgomery Fair Department Store. The rules of segregation in Montgomery at the time meant that the front of the bus was reserved for White passengers, and Black passengers had to sit in the rear. But the Montgomery laws were confusing; one interpretation held that segregation could be ignored and another stated that no Black citizen should have to give up their seat if there were others available. As a result, many Black people avoided taking the bus, but for some the bus was the only option. On this particular day, a White man boarded the bus but there was no seat available in the designated White section, so the driver told the Black passengers in the first four seats to stand and move to the "colored" section at the rear. Three of the passengers obeyed, but Rosa Parks remained in her seat. Two police officers arrested Rosa and placed her in custody.[15] Rosa Parks thus became a symbol for the Black struggle in America and would state later that Emmett Till was on her mind when she decided not to move seats.

I often think about my career in finance and capitalism in the context of these historical issues. For my mum, sister, and me, growing up without money was incredibly hard. I look at my own daughters and the advantages they have and feel the system and industry in which I operate, which is unashamedly capitalist, has played a critical role in this. But I then think about the people I grew up with and the many Black people I still see struggling. They are still socially and economically disadvantaged. Is inequality simply a feature of capitalism and thus requiring a wholesale reimagining of the system, or does it actually provide the answer?

The interactions of many Black communities, together with the version of capitalism that is part of today's modern society, do not offer much hope. Puerto Rico was initially colonized by the Spanish before the United States won control of the island in 1898. Its economy was based on agriculture and the production of sugar cane. After World War II, Luis Munoz Marin concluded that the best way to improve the economic performance was to rapidly transition away from a reliance on agriculture and industrialize through the development of a relationship with the United States. This became known as "Operation Bootstrap."[16] Many regard this as an example of success because Puerto Rico did effectively change its economy, but it's also noticeable that this created a degree of economic dependency on the United States. Puerto Rico's main trading partner is the US, which accounts for 58% of its trade.[17] Meanwhile, inequality in Puerto Rico is prevalent, with 44% of the population and 57% of children living in poverty, the vast majority of those affected being the Black communities who are descendants of the enslaved.[18] And yet this became the model on which the industrialization of the former colonies was based, as the post-slavery era of Jamaica demonstrates.

When slavery ended in Jamaica in 1834 and full freedom for the enslaved was achieved in 1938 (more than 100 years later!), the former enslaved had no land, finances, or the means to participate in the Jamaican economy, which had been established on the production and export of raw materials such as cotton and sugar to Europe.[19] As a result, many were forced into working on plantations earning subsistence wages or squatting on land, which was of poor quality. They became the peasant class, unable to earn enough money to change their circumstances and become socially mobile. This contrasted with continued trade in sugar and cotton, which helped Britain industrialize and continue its place as a world leader in both economic advancement and living standards. The 1930s global depression had a significant impact on the Caribbean, causing social unrest and resulting in a series of revolts in 1938, to which the British Government responded by appointing the Royal Commission of Inquiry. The inquiry produced a report that recommended the improvement of social services, increased financial aid, guarantees for agricultural exports, and land settlement schemes, which aimed to provide small-scale farmers with greater access to land and other resources. However, the aid package amounted to only £1million per annum over a 20-year period.[20] And, similar to the situation for Black people in the United States, these initiatives did not resolve the underlying problems of access to quality education and property and land rights.

A debate has recently begun about the type of capitalism we are living with. In 2019, executives from the world's leading businesses met at the US Business Roundtable and declared that corporations no longer exist only to serve their shareholders. It was a direct rebuke of American economist and statistician Milton Friedman and his shareholder theory. This theory has dominated the approach of Western corporations since Friedman first published his view in a 1970 *New York Times* essay. He argued that a company had no social responsibility to the public or to society; its only responsibility was to its shareholders. In 2019, the rationale for this rejection was the growing realization that developed economies, particularly the United States, have over the last 40 years experienced slowing productivity, financial shocks, and rising inequality. To answer this conundrum many authors have decried the rise of "Rentier Capitalism" — an economy in which privileged elites extract rent, such as income through intellectual, physical, or financial assets, from society. This is a mature capitalism, fully grown, independent, and able to affect the lives of millions. The concept has gathered pace following the rise of governments and movements in developed Western economies in which large swathes of these populations feel disenfranchised. If capitalism is to be part of the solution, it must evolve; otherwise, the systematic prevention of economic advancement alongside social inequality will continue.

By the time Jamaica achieved independence in 1962, the economy was still underperforming, and poverty was rife. The new government's response was to utilize the Puerto Rican example and achieve economic growth through attracting foreign investment into the country, focusing on areas of the economy such as tourism, finance, sugar, bananas, and the production of raw materials. The presence of foreign capital did little to change the fortunes of the people of Jamaica, or other former colonies. Rather, it meant that capital was increasingly transferred abroad. Jamaica proved to be an excellent investment for foreign multinationals—a capitalist economy that derived profit from the production and distribution of goods in return for profit. However, the structure of the economy maintained the formerly enslaved in their position while maximizing profits or "rents" for foreign investors.

The slave- and colonial-era dependency on a narrow set of goods like sugar, coffee, bananas, and, more recently, aluminium has stifled innovation. But it has also prevented the establishment of new markets and relationships because the purchase of these products has been dominated by the former colonists—in Jamaica's case Britain and the United States. Similarly, Jamaica became increasingly reliant on imports and foreign capital. Even today, Jamaica imports far more than it exports and had a trade deficit of US$3.49 billion in 2020, having to import raw materials such as fuel, machinery, and transport equipment.[21] This has resulted in fewer businesses that utilize domestic materials, which in turn employ and upskill local labor. Despite some gains in the reduction of public debt and unemployment, Jamaica's poverty rate was 22% in 2022.[22] This has disproportionately impacted the Black population of Jamaica in comparison to the White and Mixed former plantation owners who dominate the country's political and business elite. It also explains why my grandparents, who grew up in Jamaica, decided to travel to the UK seeking greater economic opportunities and yet found history destined to repeat itself.

In 1955, the same year Emmett Till was murdered and Rosa Parks refused to give up her seat, Winifred and Tivy boarded a ship from Jamaica to establish a new life the UK, settling in Birmingham. During the school holidays when I was growing up, we used to travel to visit my grandmother, a good 100 miles away from where we lived in London. My mother never drove, so we would catch the underground to Victoria Station before boarding a bus to Birmingham New Street. Nowadays the journey takes just over two hours by train but back then the bus would take at least three and half hours, but this was an adventure for me. I would grab a window seat and watch the landscape change from buildings as we left London, to countryside, and then back to buildings as we entered Birmingham. My grandmother lived in a three-bedroom house that was decorated in a traditional Caribbean manner. The living room was dominated by a glass cabinet with pictures of family members and glass and ceramic ornaments. Two of these stuck out particularly for me: a portrait photograph of my grandfather Tivy, whom I never met before he passed away, and a commemorative plate of the royal family, which marked the marriage of Prince Charles and Lady Diana. I wasn't sure if there was a relationship between the two items, but they seem to have pride of place in the cabinet, so clearly they were important. For many Caribbeans, moving to the UK was more than just opportunity. The UK was seen as home; Britain's long colonization of Jamaica meant any relationship that the island had to Africa had long since diminished. The British royal family were seen as Jamaica's royal family. Queen Elizabeth II was the Queen of Jamaica and Jamaica is a member of the 54 Commonwealth nations, a free association of sovereign states, former colonies that retain cooperation with Great Britain. Upon the death of Queen Elizabeth and the ascendancy of King Charles III to the throne, calls from the former colonies for greater independence have increased. It remains to be seen if this continues and changes the structure of the Commonwealth.

My grandparents were members of the "Windrush generation," economic migrants from the British Colonies who were invited to the UK to alleviate the labor shortage that was inhibiting the post–World War II recovery. The term "Windrush" comes from the fact that the first Caribbeans arrived at the Tilbury Docks on a decommissioned German warship, which had been renamed HMT *Empire Windrush*. The images of Caribbeans arriving proudly waving Union Jacks and dressed to the nines in suits, dresses, and Trilby hats as they touched down onto this new land full of opportunity became a symbol of the benefits of the British rule.

Tivy had held a skilled job as an engineer in the Jamaican national gas grid but was laid off due to a downturn that hit economically disadvantaged countries particularly hard. But when Tivy arrived in the UK, he found that his engineering skills were not transferable. Like so many skilled migrant workers then and now, he either had to retrain or be reduced to undertaking some form of manual labor. In my part-time role at a supermarket during my time at university, I worked alongside an ear, nose, and throat consultant from India. He was held in such esteem by all, including the manager of the store, that he was referred to as Mr. Choudhaury. Yet he was stacking cans of beans and jars of mustard every morning at 7 a.m. while he requalified to practice medicine.

In 1950s Britain, the situation was somewhat different. Very few Caribbeans who arrived in the UK were qualified doctors and the real labor shortage was in nursing, transportation, and construction; the idea of these groups performing other skilled roles was not entertained. Living in rented accommodations, earning minimum wage, and with limited access to quality education or healthcare meant the prospects of Black people changing their economic or social status were slim. So rather than working for British Gas, Tivy found himself working on a construction site in Aston, Birmingham. I have a big family, nine aunties and uncles who were all born two years apart from each other. The plan was to bring all the children over to provide them with greater opportunities, but my grandparents couldn't afford to bring them all at the same time. So when they had enough money, they would send for them individually, starting with the oldest, who was 18 and able to work. The money she made would be used to pay for the next sibling's ticket.

It was around this time that Tivy had a serious accident on the construction site. Health and safety standards during this period left a lot to be desired, particularly for migrant workers. My grandfather was pushing a wheelbarrow up a ramp made from a plank when it broke, and the full wheelbarrow fell on top of him. His injuries left him partially disabled, unable to work and without compensation. I often wonder how my grandfather felt about this. From the black-and-white pictures I have of him, he was a tall, handsome, and seemingly proud man. He would have felt a sense of duty. A call had come from the mothership to the former colonies, and he answered. But with the expectation of greater economic opportunity, maybe he thought this would begin to create wealth for his family? Instead, my grandmother had to provide for the family alone, working as a dressmaker in the local factory. The children who were left behind, including my mother, lived with their grandmother, my great-grandmother, but in poverty, and my grandfather died a poor man from his injuries.

3

Equity

MY MOTHER ARRIVED IN BIRMINGHAM in the UK in 1968 at age 16. She was one of nine children; she and six of her siblings were born in Jamaica but would eventually migrate to England. Her younger sister and brother were born in the UK.

This was common practice among Caribbeans who emigrated to England. My grandfather arrived first. The intention was for him to make more money than he was in Jamaica and then return home. But he simply couldn't save enough. My grandmother then joined him and helped him save enough money for their eldest daughter to emigrate. Upon arriving she began working and helped saved money for her younger sister, who arrived a couple of years later. She helped to save money for my mother's ticket. Unlike my grandparents, my mother did not make the journey across the Atlantic by sea but on a Pan Am flight, which landed at Heathrow Airport. She then caught a domestic flight to Birmingham to join her family. I asked her how she felt about making the journey. Was she anxious about moving to a new country? Nervous about getting on an airplane? She gave an emphatic "No!" It was the complete opposite; she felt nothing but excitement.

Life in Jamaica for my mother was very difficult. She was separated from her parents when they emigrated, and although she lived with her grandmother, two of her sisters, and her other brother, the poverty she experienced had a significant impact on her. Her grandmother was aging but because she had to look after four children, she still worked behind the counter at the local drugstore selling soda, sweets, and snacks. My mother recalls visiting the store after school and staying with her grandmother until she finished her shift. If she was lucky, her grandmother would sneak her a snack to eat. This was important because food was scarce; often she only ate one meal a day, which was typically a tin of sardines and "sugar water," which, as the name implies, was simply water mixed with sugar. Home was a single room shared between five people with only two beds to sleep in. My mother shared a bed with her younger sister and brother, and her grandmother shared the other bed with her other sister. Her sister eventually had a child, who also shared the bed.

In 1970, the Jamaican reggae artist Jimmy Cliff wrote the song "You Can Get It If You Really Want." I've heard the song many times; it was one of those songs that played in the background in our house as I grew up. However, I never quite realized its importance; for my mother and her generation it represented the aspiration and hopes for a better life. So there was no sadness about her leaving Jamaica; she boarded the flight with a tag on her bag that read UNACCOM-PANIED MINOR, and she was excited to be reunited with her parents after seven years of being separated, and with her brothers and sisters, two of whom she would be meeting for the first time. She was also intrigued by the prospect of a better quality of life that the economic opportunities of migrating to the UK might bring. The postwar period saw the onset of a more paternalistic capitalism and increasingly interventionist governmental social reform. These are often cited as the solution to the Black socioeconomic disadvantage, and yet we see this approach has failed to deliver.

The post–World War II period should have been a real opportunity for change for Black communities. Governments in the UK and United States undertook two social experiments: interventionist capitalism and governmental reform. Yet neither approach could break the dam that prevented Black people from progressing. In 1929 the world experienced a severe recession, which originated in the US due to a lack of consumer demand, which in turn led to a decline in production. Between its peak and through the downturn, industrial production fell by 47%.[1] It was during this period that the British economist John Maynard Keynes developed a theory to explain the Great Depression. Keynes felt that the dominant laissez-faire economic theory of the time was unable to account for the current economic malaise or to find a way out of the downturn. He published two important works, *A Treatise on Money* (1930) and *The General Theory of Employment, Interest, and Money* (1936), in which he argued against Adam Smith's classical economic theory. Smith's theory states that because the economy is free, prices and wages adjust to the ups and downs of demand over time. For example, when the economy is healthy, wages and prices increase, and when times are challenging wages and prices adjust downward. The assumption in this model is that the economy is always at full employment, so anyone who wants to work is working, and all resources are being utilized to their full capacity. The suggestion here is that if competition is allowed to work, the economy will move toward full employment, or what the economists call "potential output."

Classical economists such as Smith believed that when a recession occurs, it needs no help from anyone because the economy will self-correct. There are three issues with this when we assess this economic model through the experience of Black people. First, we need to understand the difference between equality and equity. Equality provides everyone with the same regardless of need. We typically utilize equality in the quantitative sense, as a measure of outcomes. Equity achieves equality by treating people differently based on their individual needs. An example of inequality might be the existence of measurable income disparities among different communities, while an example of inequity might be the lack of opportunities some communities face in the labor market. The debate about inequality versus inequity has been stoked in recent years. Some argue that inequity is inherent in the very fabric of society. Others argue that these do not exist. Ideologies and political beliefs are often utilized to support these views. It's difficult to "win" an ideological argument, which is why it's important to focus on the measurable outcomes. Second, we should measure inequality, but we should also understand that to reduce it will require a targeted approach depending on a community's given need. The question is what do we seek equality of—outcomes or opportunities?

Although the classical model considered slavery inefficient, Black people in the post-slavery era struggled to find employment. So the third issue is that they were often paid less when they did find work, which impacts a workforce's incentive to work more or harder. An example of creating equity could be targeted work programs to bring Black workers into the workforce. These would then be accompanied by retention plans and adequate pay. But this intervention went against free-market principles. The outcome is that economies with a significant Black population were not utilizing all resources to their full capacity.

Keynesian economics, by contrast, argued that government spending was crucial to driving demand and was necessary to maintain full employment. Keynes never defined any actual government policies, but he did believe governments should intervene to counteract the unintended consequences of the business cycle, what he termed countercyclical fiscal policies — for example, investing in infrastructure during a downturn to create jobs. Unemployment, particularly during downturns, had a severe impact on Black communities. This approach could have created equity by targeting Black workers, but again they failed to address the community's specific needs. Moreover, Black people had less accumulated wealth to draw upon and faced greater levels of unemployment when the economy contracted. So an economic theory focused on price stability and in turn full employment allowing for a more paternalistic capitalism should have been beneficial to Black people. But because these policies failed to reduce racial inequities, this had little impact on the reduction of their economic disadvantage.

In 1945, the UK emerged victorious from World War II and experienced an economic boom that lasted for 20 years. It was also an era of radical societal change. William Beveridge, a social economist, published a report in 1942 entitled "Social Insurance and Allied Services," which provided the framework for social policy in postwar Britain. Beveridge spent many years working for Toynbee Hall, a charity based in East London. Here he developed strong views about combating social inequality. His view was that philanthropy was insufficient to tackle what he called the five giants: idleness, ignorance, disease, squalor, and want. He envisioned a "cradle to grave" social program that included a free national health service. The Education Act, aimed to remove the inequalities in secondary education, was passed in 1944 and became a pillar for the postwar consensus that saw the two major political parties, Labour and Conservative, in broad agreement about the social reform. The Labour Party won a landslide majority in 1945 and undertook a significant program of nationalization of heavy industry and transport and the creation of the National Health Service.[2]

Britain's economy, however, had yet to recover from the war. The economy under Winston Churchill had been mobilized for the war effort. Some industries, such as aircraft manufacturing, were much larger than needed, while others, such as railways and mining, were in much need of investment. With rationing still very much in place, the Conservatives returned to government in 1950 and would remain for the next 13 years, first under Winston Churchill and then Anthony Eden and Harold Macmillan. Britain's postwar economic recovery began with accepting loans from the United States. The 1948 Marshall Plan was a US initiative that provided £13 billion in aid to Western Europe. It signaled a long period of US intervention in European affairs, reduced trade barriers, provided a buffer to the spread of communism, and kick-started Britain's postwar recovery. By the mid-1950s, Britain had achieved full employment. It was in this period that Prime Minister Macmillan proclaimed the people of Britain had "never had it so good."[3]

The United States adopted a similar interventionist ideology under Democratic President Franklin D. Roosevelt, who became the 32nd president during the Great Depression after defeating the Republican Herbert Hoover. World War II revived US economic fortunes and Roosevelt's government was eager to avoid the return of the 1930s depression. The New Deal was a series of programs enacted between 1933 and 1939 with the aim of providing economic relief and reforming a range of industries. These included the Agricultural Adjustment Act (AAA), the Civilian Conservation Corps (CCC), the Tennessee Valley Authority (TVA), the Federal Emergency Relief Administration (FERA), and the National Industrial Recovery Act (NIRA).[4] During the war, Roosevelt oversaw the mobilization of the US economy to support the war effort, creating the Pentagon, and the Lend-Lease Program, which supplied the Allied nations such as Great Britain and the Soviet Union with supplies to promote the defense of the United States. Roosevelt died in 1945 just before the end of the war, but his policies turned the United States into a global superpower.[5] The implementation of many New Deal policies would be overseen by Harry Truman, who became the 33rd president after Roosevelt died. Truman had his own views about social reform, and a range of policy initiatives such as national health insurance and education aid became known as the Fair Deal. At the turn of the 20th century, the American population had flocked to the country's major cities in search of employment. But after World War II, the United States underwent a phenomenon called suburbanization that saw the mass relocation of predominately White families from the inner cities to the suburbs, which were much lower in density but had the attractions of not just housing but also industrial and commercial opportunities.

Servicemen's Readjustment Act was enacted by Congress in 1944 and was designed to provide the eight million war veterans who were returning home with a degree of financial stability. The act gave war vets one year of unemployment pay after they returned home; loan guaranties to purchase their first homes, businesses, or farms; and funding for college and vocational programs. Over the next seven years, almost eight million veterans received educational benefits. Approximately 2.3 million attended college and universities, 3.5 million received school training, and 3.4 received on-the-job training. The program cost around $14.5 billion but the increase in taxes alone paid for the GI Bill several times over. By 1955, 4.3 million home loans had been granted, with a total value of $33 billion. The opportunities created by the GI Bill secured wealth for a generation, and veterans were responsible for buying 20% of all new homes built.[6]

These initiatives would provide the blueprint for the reduction of inequality in society, but within this blueprint Black people were not only left behind but the challenges they faced were exacerbated. Although there was increased government intervention in the economy, Black people consistently occupied low-wage, service-oriented roles with little opportunity for wealth creation. When my mother arrived in the UK at 16, like many Caribbeans she did not continue her formal education; rather, she immediately began working in a clothing factory in Aston, Birmingham. She was living with one of her older sisters and she had to pay her way; the priority was therefore earning money. Although the money my mother earned was significantly more than she could earn in Jamaica, she was working in service-orientated roles at low wages with little opportunity for progression. Black people were needed to fulfill a role in the postwar recovery and any personal aspirations they may have had were secondary.

My mother was also obliged to send home a proportion of the money she earned to help her younger sister purchase a ticket to the UK, so her opportunity to save was limited. The focus on earning money, rather than on education, meant there was limited opportunity to upskill and increase her earning power. Her housing was better than her grandmother's one-bedroom place in Jamaica, but with no earning power, the prospect of purchasing a home or moving to an area with increased job prospects was out of the question. So she rented accommodation but often with no amenities such as heating or electricity.

Financing to create wealth was also difficult during this period because the banks were reluctant to lend to Black people. When they did gain loans, they were often charged at a higher rate, an example of socioeconomic disadvantage and societal discrimination preventing economic progress. This did result in some very innovative solutions, such the creation of the first credit unions, a bank that is fully owned and operated by the customers as a cooperative. The first of these was established in 1964, the Hornsey Co-operative Credit Union, as 10 pioneers from the Ferme Park Baptist Church sought to find an alternative method of financing property purchases. By 1974, Britain had 48 credit unions with 39,000 members, around two-thirds of whom were of West Indian origin.[7] However, this did not resolve the discrimination Black people faced from banking institutions, nor did it create trust in the mainstream system. Black entrepreneurs still struggle to raise adequate financing today. The ripples travel decades. For my mother this was still better than life in Jamaica, but once she adjusted to life in England she began to realize how disadvantaged she was and improving her quality of life further would be incredibly difficult. As Jimmy Cliff wrote, "You've got your mind set on a dream/ You can get it though hard it may seem now."

Before the onset of the Great Depression, many Black Americans still worked in the South as sharecroppers or tenant farmers, their poor economic and social conditions persisting in the face of their inability to pay off debts and accumulate wealth. Many migrated to cities such as New York, Philadelphia, Los Angeles, and Oakland but found themselves working as domestic servants or laborers. The South had always suffered challenging economic conditions due to rapid industrialization, but the 1929 stock market crash meant Black workers were the first to be let go from their positions, often without any accumulated wealth to fall back on. White unemployment averaged 25% in 1932. But Black unemployment reached 50% in Chicago and Pittsburgh, 60% in Philadelphia and Detroit, and in Atlanta 70% were jobless by 1934.[8] Given the social and economic imperative of Roosevelt's New Deal, this impact on the economic situation of Black people could have been positive, and initiatives such as the Public Works Administration (PWA), which oversaw the construction of thousands of housing projects aimed at poor Black communities in areas such as New York, Atlanta, and Philadelphia, also ensured construction crews had to employ Black workers in proportion to the local population. But many of the other New Deal initiatives exacerbated existing problems. The AAA and the TVA were predominately implemented in the agricultural South, but without adequate oversight they quickly became discriminatory. For example, in the 1920s Southern farmers produced too much supply for the US market, which caused prices to fall. The AAA was created to implement a "domestic allotment plan" to raise the price of farm products by paying famers to produce less. However, it had a disproportionate impact on Black sharecroppers as landowners simply evicted them off the land. Similarly, the Social Security Act, which granted unemployment insurance and retirement benefits to workers, was amended by Southern congressional representatives to exclude farmers and domestic workers from being eligible. The result was 87% of all Black women and 55% of all Black workers were excluded.[9]

In contrast to White soldiers, the 1.2 million Black soldiers who had fought against racism and bigotry abroad were subject to racism within the ranks of the US Army. The Jim Crow laws, still very prevalent in the United States, segregated White and Black soldiers; many Black servicemembers were treated as second-class citizens despite fighting for their country.

Upon their return home from the war, they were denied the benefits of the GI Bill. Although the bill did not specifically exclude Black Americans, its implementation was discriminatory. A report issued by the Department of Veterans Affairs stated that Black veterans could not access the benefits through the GI Bill because only those who had been given honorable discharge were eligible. Black soldiers found themselves much more likely to be given dishonorable discharge and often this was due to outright discrimination.[10] Those who did qualify were unable to participate in vocational educational programs such as plumbing and electricity because equipment was only available to White students. There were protests when Black veterans tried to move into now-White neighborhoods; benefits such as unemployment and insurance were given to White claimants ahead of Black claimants. Though the GI Bill guaranteed loans for home purchases, it was the responsibility of White-owned financial institutions to administer them, and Black applicants were often refused. Redlining was a practice of deploying financial services like lending and insurance to neighborhoods defined by race, color, and income. Color-coded maps showed areas outlined in red, and financial services were often limited or was applied arbitrarily for those in the areas within the red lines. This meant it was more challenging for Black people to purchase homes.

The other route to increase social mobility was through education, but again many Black veterans were unable to take advantage of this aspect of the GI Bill. They needed to work rather than study and they had limited ability to access White educational institutions, both in the North and, particularly, in the South. The only route for many, therefore, were local Black educational institutions that were chronically underfunded, under-resourced, and simply unable to cater to the thousands of applicants. It was this that increased the wealth gap between White and Black people, not just the community's social status but a systematic denial of access to the resources and opportunities that could fundamentally improve their economic position.[11] If classical capitalism espoused by Adam Smith failed to raise the prospects for Black people, perhaps Keynesian interventionist governmental policies could. Yet we see that these failed to get to the root of the issue.

At a meeting of the Conservative Political Centre on April 20, 1968, a Conservative MP called Enoch Powell gave an infamous speech that became known as the "Rivers of Blood" speech. It focused on mass immigration and the impact on the White population, and opposed a piece of legislation called the Race Relations Bill:

They found their wives unable to obtain hospital beds in childbirth, their children unable to obtain school places, their homes and neighbourhoods changed beyond recognition, their plans and prospects for the future defeated; at work they found that employers hesitated to apply to the immigrant worker the standards of discipline and competence required of the native-born worker; they began to hear, as time went by, more and more voices which told them that they were now the unwanted. . . . We must be mad, literally mad, as a nation to be permitting the annual inflow of some 50,000 dependents, who are for the most part the material of the future growth of the immigrant descended population. It is like watching a nation busily engaged in heaping up its own funeral pyre. So insane are we that we actually permit unmarried persons to immigrate for the purpose of founding a family with spouses and fiancées whom they have never seen. . . . On top of this, they now learn that a one-way privilege is to be established by Act of Parliament; a law which cannot, and is not intended to, operate to protect them or redress their grievances, is to be enacted to

give the stranger, the disgruntled and the agent provocateur the
power to pillory them for their private actions.[12]

Interestingly, Powell was a believer in free-market capitalism, which at the time was a fringe movement in the
Conservative Party but would come to dominate the party's
policy under Margaret Thatcher. Powell's opponents found it
difficult to reconcile his aversion to immigration with his
views on the free market for which the free movement of
labor was advantageous. But what they failed to recognize
was that this was the beginning of a pattern of three features
of British society: an increase in racial tension alongside economic instability, migrants being targeted when Britain's
sovereignty is challenged, and the pitting of poor White people against even poorer Black people.

The 1960s saw a decline in Britain's status as an international superpower. In 1956, Egyptian president Gamal Abdel
Nasser nationalized the Suez Canal. In response, Israel, and
then France and Britain, invaded Egypt to regain control of
the canal, a strategically important trading route. After political pressure from the United States, the United Nations, and
the Soviet Union, the three invaders withdrew from the
region.[13] For Britain this was a national embarrassment. By
1960 Macmillan stated that the "wind of change" was blow-
ing through Africa, signaling an end to colonial rule in Africa
and other nations. In 1964 Labour was reelected under the
leadership of Harold Wilson, regarded as a progressive, and
the death penalty was abolished, homosexuality decriminal-
ized, and society began to undergo a fundamental change in
attitudes and beliefs. But by 1968, the postwar recovery was
slowing down and Britain began to experience a rise in inequality that also impacted the White population. So anti-
immigration become an outlet for this dissatisfaction, a pattern
we will see repeated.

I asked my mother if she was aware of this when she arrived in the country. She said the "Rivers of Blood" speech was a huge news story at the time. I was also intrigued about her relationship with her White co-workers. Was there a peaceful co-existence or any antagonism? My mother stated that initially she felt no animosity; her White colleagues were very cordial. She only realized there was a difference when she saw one of her White colleagues outside the factory and attempted to greet her with a smile; the women looked at her, recognized her, but then deliberately ignored her. Although the UK needed Black people economically, socially there was tension. My mother became increasingly aware of her lower social status; this was the era of "No Irish, No Blacks No Dogs." An often neglected part of Black British history is that it had its own Civil Rights Movement. This was led by the likes of Paul Stephenson, who in 1963 led a boycott against the Bristol bus company that barred Black and Asian people from boarding buses.[14] My mother was active in these protests; in one of my favorite pictures of her she is sporting an afro, which itself was a visual protest against the oppression Black people felt at this time. Although, this wasn't universal; when her sister saw my mother's afro she said, "You're not going out with your hair like that!?" But this was the period of "I'm Black and Proud," reclaiming an identity and making it a virtue. She and my father felt compelled to change their circumstances and those of others, and they listened to the likes of US activists such as Angela Davis, who campaigned for women's rights, civil rights, and against the Vietnam War.

In 1963, Dr. Martin Luther King Jr. delivered his famous "I Have a Dream" speech to more than 250,000 civil rights supporters during the March on Washington for Jobs and Freedom. It was a call for equality for Black Americans. Civil rights are defined as the rights of citizens to political and social freedoms and equality; this was certainly a demand made by activists. A series of civil disobedience acts as political and social protests did result in more equality. In Greensboro, North Carolina, in 1960, hundreds of protestors staged a sit-in after four Black college students were refused service at a Woolworths lunch counter. In 1961 seven Black and six White activists boarded a Greyhound bus and embarked in a tour of the US South to protest against the segregated bus terminals.[15] The protests soon spanned every aspect of Black lives, including the iconic picture of athletes Tommie Smith and John Carlos holding up their fists in a Black Power salute at the 1968 Olympics.

The Civil Rights era of the 1960s should be seen as a watershed moment in history; it made discrimination unlawful. Under the US Civil Rights Act of 1964, signed by President Lyndon B. Johnson, segregation on the grounds of race, religion, or national origin was banned at all places of public accommodation, including restaurants, parks, hotels, and sports venues. It was followed by the Voting Rights Act of 1965, which outlawed discriminatory voting practices such as literacy tests. The Fair Housing Act of 1968 banned discrimination in the sale, rental, or financing of property.[16] The 1974 Equal Educational Opportunities Act stated no US state can deny equal educational opportunity to any person based on gender, race, color, or nationality through intentional segregation.[17] In the UK, the Race Relations Act was passed in 1965 and was strengthened by the 1968 Race Relations Act. Both outlawed discrimination on the grounds of color, race, or ethnic origins in public and eventually employment and housing. These were superseded and repealed by the 1976 Race Relations Act that prevented discrimination on the grounds of race, color, nationality, cthnic, and national origin in employment and in the provision of goods and services, education, and public functions.[18]

However, these significant steps forward did not change the socioeconomic complex. Making a discriminatory act unlawful cannot change beliefs or values that still manifest in social attitudes or behaviors. Nor did they remove or change the economic barriers to progression. Social stratification had placed Black people at the bottom of society that had been systematically developed over 250 years of slavery, 100 years of Jim Crow, and 100 years of colonialism. Real change needs to address both the social and economic barriers that exist and then systematically break through them in a coordinated approach. As Jimmy Cliff wrote, "Persecution you must bear/Win or lose you got to get your share." Share denotes ownership, a stake in society but also in the economy. In 1966, Martin Luther King Jr. wrote an article for the *Nation* in which he acknowledges the policy decisions that have been made but also goes on to state:

> *The future is more complex. Slums with hundreds of thousands of living units are not eradicated as easily as lunch counters or buses are integrated. Jobs are harder to create than voting rolls. Harmonizing of peoples of vastly different cultural levels is complicated and frequently abrasive. . . . It is easy to conceive of a plan to raise the minimum wage and thus in a single stroke extract millions of people from poverty. But between the conception and the realization there lies a formidable wall. Someone has been profiting from the low wages of Negroes. Depressed living standards for Negroes are a structural part of the economy. Certain industries are based upon the supply of low-wage, underskilled and immobile nonwhite labor. Hand assembly factories, hospitals, service industries, housework, agriculture operations using itinerant labor, would all suffer shock, if not disaster, if the minimum wage were significantly raised. A hardening of opposition to the satisfaction of Negro needs must be anticipated as the movement presses against financial privilege.*

These views were formalized in Dr. King's fourth and final book before his assassination, *Where Do We Go From Here: Chaos or Community?* (1967). In it he asserts that yes, Black people have a degree of social and political freedom, but these cannot be realized until there is genuine economic reform. Dr. King's idea? Guaranteed income.

In 1973, the postwar boom truly came to end with a global recession that differed from others. Developed economies suffered high unemployment and inflation at the same time, a concept known as stagflation. This was caused by the 1973 oil crisis and President Richard Nixon's attempts to control increasing inflation through price freezes and surcharges on imports, which effectively ended an era of international monetary coordination known as the Bretton Woods system. During this period, it is estimated that 2.3 million jobs were lost; this would preoccupy the presidencies of Gerald Ford and Jimmy Carter.

In the UK, GDP declined by 3.9% and Conservative Prime Minister Edward "Ted" Heath declared a three-day week after the threat of power shortages due to widespread strikes by coal miners. Heath offered a 13% pay rise to the miners but this was rejected. He then called a snap election to decide who really ran the country. The result was a hung parliament and when he failed to create a coalition with the Liberal Party, he was forced to resign. This allowed Labour under Harold Wilson to form a minority government in 1974.

Britain returned to economic growth in 1975 but inflation remained high. James Callaghan, who replaced Harold Wilson, had to navigate a series of strikes between 1978 and 1979 known as the "Winter of Discontent"[19] My mother remembers this period vividly, not least because my sister and I were born in 1975 and 1977. Discussing this period with my mother was fascinating, but it also served as warning. At the time she felt the world was on the cusp of seismic change. However, we also realized that history tends to repeat itself;

this wouldn't be the first time the death of a Black person would result in protest and the veneer of reform would occur. So we both questioned what has really changed. To really progress, *wanting it* might not be enough. My mother's experience raising a son and a daughter, on her own, during an economic boom while Black communities rioted would provide more questions than answers.

4

Horses and Sparrows

I WATCHED AS THE BALL was kicked high into the air. It was late summer, so although it was early, the setting sun meant the floodlights on the football pitch (soccer field) were lit, silhouetting the ball against the glaring light. There must have been about three or four of us. We weren't playing a match, just passing the ball to one another to see who had the best control. In that moment of watching the ball create an arc in the sky, I was happy, not thinking about the past or the future, not really thinking at all. Which is why I didn't see them coming.

A punch in the stomach doubled me over and I wheezed to the ground; for a moment, everything was still, almost serene. Then the pain crawled up my back like a spider, entered my brain, then slid down to my front, where it finally registered. Then the kicks started, raining down on me. With no breath, all I could do was curl into a ball. It seemed to last forever, although it was probably only a matter of seconds and then it stopped. "Gavin, Gavin . . . are you OK? Get up now. . . ." One of the playscheme teachers had broken things up and then helped me get to my feet. Funded by local councils, typically in inner-city areas of London, playschemes were designed to provide activities for children during school holidays. They were run by playscheme leaders, or "teachers" as we called them.

As I straightened up, I saw three boys staring at me; the playscheme teacher was standing between us. The two other boys I was playing football with were standing to the side, watching events unfold. "So what happened?" the teacher asked. I blurted out, "I didn't do anything, I was just playing football!" One of the boys then said, "He thinks he's flash." "Flash" was '80s slang for "show-off." Today I don't recall who the other boys were or even what they looked like, but I do remember the boy who spoke. He had a short unkempt afro and eyes that were slightly too close together, which gave him a menacing look. Despite the fact that I had been attacked, the teacher simply told us to stay apart. Fights were an everyday occurrence; to get to the bottom of every single one would have been nigh on impossible.

Summer holidays were the longest of the school holidays and they were usually spent at one of these playschemes. Kids from different schools were thrust together and tensions often ran high. For the parents, these centers were vital because many were working and could not afford any other childcare. For the kids, they kept us off the streets and out of trouble. But the ratio of children to teachers was often very high. I dreaded going to the playschemes; they were often different from year to year, with different kids and new relationships to establish. Too often this meant having to prove myself physically. This was particularly hard for me because, though I was tall for my age, I was skinny, wore glasses, and had "goofy" teeth. I might as well have had a target on my back, and many times it felt like I did. It was rare that I knew many other kids at these playschemes. Some were lucky to have schoolfriends, who often created cliques to survive, or an older brother who had a name. I had neither and as a result there was often a "testing phase" where the other kids would establish where you were in the pecking order. Given that I had had no interaction with the three boys before being attacked, it was clear this was the reason for the violence.

A few days later I was again playing football. This time it was the middle of the day, and the summer sun was beating down on me. Across from the football pitch there was a large patch of grass and a fallen tree trunk, which I assume was placed there on purpose. It doubled as a bench and a boundary for when a six was hit when we played cricket. Behind it was a fence that separated the playscheme from the street to keep us safe, protecting us from the outside world. Or maybe it was to keep us in. I heard shouting kids running toward the fence, then a familiar cry of "Fight, fight!" This was a siren call to an altercation, and the usual response was for kids to swarm around to get a glimpse of the action.

There was never any help from the spectators. If you were in the fight, it now simply meant you had an audience, and the stakes became incredibly high. Win the fight and your stock would rise; this was credibility and often the only form of status you could gather. Lose and you would be ridiculed, or worse, be seen as easy prey for other kids wanting to raise their social status. As a result, arguments often escalated incredibly quickly. An exchange of a few words would often lead to bystanders stopping to see how things would play out. A disagreement about something benign, such as whether a goal should stand, would become a confrontation. I remember being in these situations and desperately not wanting to fight. I could also see the unwillingness to fight in my opponent, but neither I nor he could afford to back down.

One fight involved a boy I had befriended and felt close to. The older kids were constantly asking who would win a fight,

Gavin or Ian? So when I accidently fouled Ian during a game of football, it didn't take much for the other kids to say, "Are you gonna take that, Ian?" It placed both of us in an impossible situation. When you're in a fight, time seems to slow down, so those few minutes felt like an age. Yet when it was over, it was hard to recall much of what happened, though the metallic taste of blood and the smell of dirt or grass make certain aspects incredibly vivid. Unless you decisively beat up the other kid, the crowd would score the bout and you would have to deal with the ignominy of statements such as, "I can't believe you let him do that to you" or "You couldn't even beat up Ian."

On this particular day, it wasn't me who was fighting, but four boys fighting one another. The scene felt familiar, except that it was happening outside of the playscheme on the other side of the fence. I couldn't quite make out who they were or even really see what was going on because the crowd had grown quite large. So I placed myself at the edge of the melee. At first the sound of the playscheme teachers telling us to get away from the fence broke through the shouting. Then there was the faint noise of police sirens in the distance and an "oohh" from the crowd. I didn't see what caused the fight, but I did see the tooth that left the mouth of one of the boys and rolled up just by me outside the fence. The police sirens grew louder as the playscheme teachers started dragging people away. I got a clearer look at the scene and it was the same boy who had led the attack against me. He looked so much smaller this time, tears streaming down his face, a visible gap in his mouth where his tooth was missing, and a lot of blood. I felt no satisfaction from this. I felt the opposite—I understood what he was going through. I hadn't seen the three boys who were beating him up before. At the time they looked old but couldn't have been more than 12 or 13. And yet these were the lessons I was learning at age 8.

The 1980s were a distinctive time in history. Culturally this was the era of rampant masculinity. Our heroes were Sylvester Stallone and Arnold Schwarzenegger; Rambo and the Terminator were the icons we aspired to be. My favorite toy was He-Man, an overly muscled superhero who would rescue his planet from the supervillain Skeletor. Then, as now, pop culture was merely a reflection of society and its institutions.

Ronald Reagan was born on February 6, 1911, in Tampico, Illinois, the second child of Nelle and John Reagan. He studied economics and sociology at college but a screen test in 1937 saw him awarded a Hollywood contract; he went on to feature in over 50 films. Reagan's early political views were liberal, but he become heavily involved in the film industry's anti-communist movement, which swept the United States during the height of the Cold War. As president of the Screen Actors Guild, he became a spokesperson for conservatism. In 1966, he was elected governor of California and was reelected in 1970. In 1980, Reagan won the Republican presidential nomination and chose United Nations Ambassador George H. W. Bush as his running mate against the Democratic incumbent president, Jimmy Carter. Against a backdrop of government intervention in the economy and inflation, Reagan became the 40th president of the United States by winning 489 electoral votes with Carter winning only 49.[1]

Margaret Thatcher was born on October 13, 1925, in Grantham, Lincolnshire, the daughter of Alfred Roberts, a grocer and alderman, and Beatrice Ethel Stephenson. Thatcher studied chemistry at Oxford University, where her interest in politics led to her appointment as the first woman president of the Oxford University Conservative Association. After a brief career as a chemist, she qualified as a barrister before entering politics in 1959 through winning the "safe" conservative seat of Finchley in North London. Thatcher rose rapidly through the party ranks, serving as a parliamentary secretary for the Ministry of Pensions and National Insurance from 1961 to 1974, chief opposition spokesman on education and science from 1969 to 1970, and secretary of state for education and science in Heath's government from 1970 to 1974. After Prime Minister Heath lost two successive elections in 1974, Thatcher was the only minister to challenge for the party leadership and, with the support of the party's right wing, she was elected as the first woman leader of a major political party in 1975.[2] Thatcher then led the Conservatives to electoral victory in 1979 in the aftermath of the Winter of Discontent.

Reagan and Thatcher would change the face of the United States and the UK. Reaganism and Thatcherism represented a sharp departure from the Keynesian model of capitalism and its central tenets of government regulation of the economy, big welfare state, and nationalization of industries. Philosophically, Thatcherism and Reaganism were characterized by a belief in neoliberal individualism. In 1987, Thatcher famously stated there is no such thing as society. "There are individual men and women and there are families. And no government can do anything except through people, and people must look after themselves first."[3] Supporters argued this ensured human rights were protected and created a culture of personal responsibility rather than a culture of dependency on the state. This belief had a significant influence on government policy. Reaganism was characterized by reduced taxation, reduced social spending, the deregulation of the markets, and increased military spending. Thatcherism ended the British postwar consensus and espoused a belief in free-market economics, minimal government spending, and privatization of industry.

Both ideologies also heralded the arrival of a more muscular capitalism, a capitalism that would find a way out of economic stagnation and increase prosperity for all based on the concept of trickle-down economics. This theory holds that taxes on businesses and the wealthy should be reduced to stimulate economic growth. Canadian economist John Kenneth Galbraith, a critic of supply-side economics, used a phrase to describe this theory: *If you feed enough oats to the horse, some with pass through to feed the sparrows.*[4] This theory is based on two key assumptions: that businesses and the wealthy are in the best position to stimulate growth, and that this will have a positive impact on society, reducing inequality. Real GDP did grow under Reagan, with an annual compound growth rate of GDP of 3.6% compared to 2.7% during the preceding eight years.[5] And under Thatcher, GDP rose by 29.4%, an average of 0.6% per quarter.[6] But when I reflect upon this period, I'm struck by a number of issues.

The first is that it is very difficult to assess how equal or unequal the UK and United States were by these measures alone. For example, Britain experienced two severe recessions during the Thatcher years. In an attempt to control inflation, Thatcher instituted a range of monetarist polices such as privatization of state-owned assets, deregulation of industries such as finance, higher interest rates, and reduced taxes and spending cuts. These policies did reduce inflation but led to a fall in output. So although inflation was reduced to 5%, by 1983 this was accompanied by over three million unemployed as traditional industries such as mining and manufacturing were shut down.

Another way of looking at inequality is through the Lorenz curve and the Gini coefficient. The Lorenz curve was developed by Max O. Lorenz in 1905 and is a method of showing the distribution of income within an economy. If there was perfect equality—meaning everyone had the same level of income—the poorest 20% of the population would gain 20% of total income or the poorest 40% would gain 40% of total income. We can use this to assess income disparities; for example, it might be that in an economy the poorest 20% might only have 10% of total income and the richest 10% might have 50% of total income. The Lorenz curve can be used to measure different levels of inequality through the Gini coefficient.[7] This is a number that measures disparities in income. So if the number is 1, it means wealth is concentrated in the hands of one person, while a measure of 0% means wealth is shared equally. During the Thatcher era, the Gini coefficient increased from 0.25% in 1979 to 0.34% by the early 1990s.[8] Thatcher famously stated that she didn't care about the gap between rich and poor, but rather that everyone became better off in absolute terms. "So as long as the gap is smaller, they'd rather have the poor poorer." Jonathan Jones in the *Spectator* argued that after taking into account house price inflation, the income of the 10th percentile fell by 2.4%, meaning the poor were worse off in 1990 than in 1979.

Similarly, Reagan also took office amid challenging economic conditions. The United States was experiencing stagflation, a phenomenon where inflation and unemployment are both high. Some attributed this to the polices of Paul Volcker, the Federal Reserve chair, who attempt to control inflation by keeping interest rates high. A consequence of higher interest rates can be a restriction in lending and investment. This can lower inflation but, as we see with the UK, can lead to high unemployment. US unemployment would reach 11% by 1982, and the rate of poverty would increase from 11.7% to 15%.[9] Similarly the Gini coefficient was 0.40% in 1980 but had reached 0.42% by 1990.[10]

There are drawbacks to the Gini coefficient, however. In reality, it really only measures how widespread income is distributed. It does not measure individual incomes, nor does it take into account the income of different countries.

Measuring income only does not account for gender, age, or ethnic differences, nor does it measure productivity or wealth. And where these can be measured, they rarely take into account cultural influences or societal factors. This has a number of repercussions.

We must first question why we don't have a more accurate measure of inequality. Governments, institutions, and individuals are able to take action against a variety of issues because they are measured and assessed. Central banks measure inflation through the rate of increase in prices and can take action if the numbers move above a certain rate. Insurers measure longevity through life expectancy and adjust premiums accordingly. If we can do this, how can we also understand the magnitude of the problem and how much it impacts a country's economy and society?

Secondly, without an adequate measure it is impossible to truly assess any attempts to reduce inequality as we are forced to rely on anecdotal evidence. If anything did trickle down to us, it wasn't tangible. As a child you really have no reference for your circumstances; whether you are rich or poor, your life is all you know. There were, of course, events that today I remember. I am amazed how my mother managed to feed and clothe us on nothing but state benefits. I always had the cheapest sneakers, which was an issue when your place in the hierarchy was often dependent on what you wore on your feet. I would turn the pages of the shopping catalogue and gaze longingly at the high-end Nike Airs and would wonder what impact this would have on my status. But on reflection what I really felt was a distinct feeling of unease, that we were living on a knife edge, that if my mum were unable to make ends meet, the consequences would be dire.

But perhaps the biggest issue is that without a more robust measure, we fail to understand the impact of the intersection of social and economic factors. Social disadvantage is typically characterized by our social interactions, by the way individuals or segments of society either react to us or treat us. These negative interactions can be incredibly damaging, the cumulative effect causing deep mental and physical harm. But it is the social disadvantage that compounds the economic disadvantage that I feel is the most overlooked.

The UK Housing Act of 1980 gave millions of council tenants in England and Wales the "Right to Buy" their house from their local authority. Many went on to purchase their homes and benefitted from the UK's rapid housing price inflation. In 1980 the US Congress passed the Depository Institutions Deregulation and Monetary Control Act, which deregulated financial institutions by partly repealing the 1932 Glass-Steagall Act, which separated retail and commercial banking.[11] This allowed for much greater innovation and reflected Reagan's belief in Milton Friedman's shareholder capitalism. In the UK, this took the form of the "Big Bang," in which Thatcher, through an agreement with the London Stock Exchange, deregulated the UK banking system to rival that of the US deregulation. This abolished minimum fixed commissions on trades, which allowed greater competition. It ended the separation of dealers and advisors, which allowed a surge in mergers and acquisitions and allowed overseas firms to own UK brokers, which in turn opened London's market to international banks.[12] Those working in the sector suddenly found themselves at the helm of a booming and incredibly lucrative industry and the wealth generated during this period was immortalized in films such as Oliver Stone's 1987 *Wall Street*, which starred Michael Douglas as the "Greed is good" Gordon Gekko, and the UK "yuppie" caricature.

By contrast, many UK Black families were reluctant to purchase their homes. This was due to a longstanding mistrust of the finance system and their inability to gain access to banking services when they first arrived in the country. This is an economic issue that manifests socially. Similarly, many Black graduates didn't know the financial services industry existed, and those who did were hesitant to apply because they didn't feel it was a place for them. Even if they did apply, many struggled to gain employment in the sector because they didn't fit the archetype. Again, this is an economic issue that presents socially. Those who were on the outside, through a lack of knowledge or a lack of access, missed out on some of the biggest opportunities for wealth creation in a generation.

If we are to create a measure for inequality and find solutions, it must therefore traverse the intersection between social and economic disadvantage, particularly those that limit horizons of Black people and other people's expectations of us. This means understanding the importance of recognition, the physical environment, and education.

Philosophers have spent years discussing the importance of recognition. The earliest proponent was Georg Wilhelm Friedrich Hegel, who was heavily influenced by another philosopher, Johann Gottlieb Fichte. In his work *The Phenomenology of Spirit* (1807), Hegel argues that we become conscious beings not through self-reflection or introspection but only through interacting with others. He builds on this idea in *Elements of the Philosophy of Right* (1820), where he argues recognition is the process through which our existence as social and political beings is created and successful integration in society is dependent upon receiving and then giving adequate recognition. So think of the reverence we might bestow upon a doctor and the sense of worth they achieve not only from helping others but also from their place in society.

On the other hand, a lack of recognition in society can destroy a person's relationship with themself and with others. This idea of misrecognition was explored by Frantz

Fanon, who described the severe physiological harm felt by victims of racism and colonialism. Fanon was born on the island of Martinique under French colonial rule and in 1952, at just 27, he published his first major work, *Black Skin, White Masks*. In this, Fanon tackled a range of issues from the perspective of a Black person under colonial rule. Fanon was hugely influenced by Hegel, and he agreed that an individual's existence only is realized when they interact with others. But unlike Hegel, Fanon believed that White masters do not need to interact with Blacks who were enslaved to achieve recognition. Because they are merely cheap labor, conversely the enslaved do not achieve recognition; rather they are maintained in their position as subordinates. It is this misrecognition that leads to Black people being seen and internalizing their position as inferior human beings.

More recently these ideas were developed by contemporary commentators. Charles Taylor published an essay entitled "Multi-Culturalism and the Politics of Recognition" (1992). Taylor argued that within the political sphere there is a demand for recognition and it is this that drove the feminist and race movements, particularly in the 1960s. Taylor believed that recognition is a vital human need, that identity is "partly shaped by recognition or its absence," and that "Nonrecognition or misrecognition can inflict harm, can be a form of oppression, imprisoning someone in a false, distorted and reduced mode of being." Francis Fukuyama describes this as Thymos (2014) as the part of the human soul that craves recognition, and in a similar vein to Fanon felt this is behind many great uprisings, from the French Revolution to the feminism and civil rights movements.

Much of the debate surrounding Fanon centers on his views on violence as a means to overcome colonial oppression, which he articulated in *The Wretched of the Earth*

(1961), a discussion about the impact of colonialism through the experience of French-colonized Algeria. Critics of Taylor focus on the rise of identity politics as negative and divisive. But when I reflect on their views, I can't help but see my experiences living in the inner city as intertwined with a struggle for recognition. We might not be enslaved, but society—whether explicitly or implicitly—tells us we are less. This might be through the treatment received by figures of authority or lack of role models in the professional world. To benefit from any opportunities afforded by Thatcherism and Reaganism would have required the aspiration to look outward, into the world, and believe we have a place there. But we couldn't. We didn't even know the outside world existed, so we looked inwardly and our search for recognition made us turn on each other, maintaining our current status, occupying the bottom rung of society.

When you grow up in the circumstances I did, it's difficult to understand there are alternative ways to gain recognition. The physical environment in which many Black people grow up also limit horizons. The term "ghetto" is derived from the Venetian verb *gettare,* meaning to pour or to cast. This marked the presence of a copper foundry located in Jewish district of Venice in the 16th century. Venice had confined its Jewish population to a northern part of the city and by the 17th and 18th centuries, other Jewish districts located in Rome and Florence also became known as *ghettos.* The Jewish emancipation began in the 18th century and this saw the dissolution of many of the ghettos. But the name lived on. Large Jewish neighborhoods in Manhattan were often referred to as the New York ghetto, and the forced segregation of the Jews during the Nazi regime saw the term utilized again. So the term "ghetto" did not become synonymous with Black neighborhoods until the early 20th century, when the Black communities in the United States were effectively segregated.[13] Redlining not only increased the wealth gap by denying finance, insurance, and access to adequate health-care and education, but it also denied the belief or aspiration that the world beyond your immediate vicinity was for you.

This was partly driven by the physical environment. In London, many ghettos were populated by state- or council-run public housing, most of which was built during the post–World War II reconstruction and was initially greeted positively. My mother was living with two young children in one room, which soon became too small. As a single parent she was able apply for public housing and was given a "tour" of a council estate in Tottenham. The estate had distinctive red bricks and was designed as a square, with four adjoining blocks and balconies overlooking a playground so parents could keep a watchful eye on their children. It was an attractive place to live, with local shops, schools, and a high street just a short walk away.

For the first few years we enjoyed living in Tottenham. I have fond memories of visiting the local parks as a family. There was also a sense of community as I attended the local school, which meant friends were never far away. We also had family living close by and would see our cousins most weekends. After a few years, however, a lack of investment into inner-city areas such as Tottenham impacted the local community. This is an important distinction to make. Many people assume such inner-city areas are almost inherently troubled. They're not. They are full of hard-working people who wish to progress, but without opportunity this becomes difficult. The children's playground we could see from our apartment soon became run down. The windows on the other side of the buildings that looked to the outside world were tiny by comparison; it always felt to me that we were forced to look inwards, over this playground, imprisoned so our worlds started and ended here. I remember vividly the dank elevator that felt like a death trap, the caretaker who sprayed bleach to hide the smell of urine, and the dogs who barked all night. We also noticed that a majority of the residents were Black. When my mother was offered the property, she could have refused it and asked to see another, and maybe have been presented with a house. But she had no idea that this right existed. It was only after taking her children to schools and mixing with the White parents that she realized they all lived a little farther away and had a lot more space.

Rappers have often discussed the built environment in their lyrics. In "N.Y. State of Mind Part II," released in 2011 and a sequel to his 1994 original, US rapper Nas states:

Broken glass in the hallway, blood-stained floors
Neighbors, look at every bag you bring through your doors
Lock the top lock, momma shoulda cuffed me to the radiator
Why not? It might've saved later from my block

In "Council Estate of Mind," released in 2004 in part as a tribute to Nas, UK rapper Skinnyman states:

I live amongst smashed syringes,
Squatters' doors hangin' off the hinges,
Hookers lookin' money for Bobby, shottin' their minges.
Leavin' used condoms out on the staircases,
Next to the broken pipes that's left by the Base Heads.
Local estate heads, have grown up to hate Feds,
Kids with no helmets drivin' round on some bait peds.

As I grew older, this playground became a cricket and football pitch and eventually a gladiatorial arena overlooked by viewing galleries and where it often felt like I was fighting for my life.

And when you're a sparrow in such a small world, an inch becomes a mile. Many assume Black people are prone to violence, as this is something innate. Marginalized groups still require recognition, but their choice of how this is achieved is greatly reduced. For us it was often physical: who was the strongest, fastest, best with girls; then it became material: who has the best clothes and trainers. There was no other example of another identity available, so this is what you aspired to become. The issue is therefore one of poverty, with both poor White and Brown communities experiencing poor physical and mental health and higher rates of crime due to their circumstances—circumstances brought about by economic conditions and the society that keeps them there. As I grew older, this didn't change. Instead, the stakes became higher: fights with fists became fights with knives. There were some who seemed to embrace this; they adapted to this life and were good at it, though the real sadness is that their potential was so much greater.

I was never "hard" but had to pretend to be as a form of self-protection. On one occasion, again a summer holiday, I was with a group of friends and we took a trip to another council estate about a 15-minute walk away. When we arrived, we saw a familiar face, another boy we went to school with. We were never close friends but we were never enemies. Yet when he saw me, the air simply filled with tension. He greeted everyone except me and then made some comments about my sneakers. My friends and I eventually departed but I knew the situation was primed to escalate.

A few days later, someone in our group suggested we visit the same estate again. I said I wasn't keen but was instantly called out for being scared about not wanting to see the same boy. Looking back on it, I recognize that the boy in my group wanted to see a fight. I clearly didn't but felt trapped, so off we went. I knew something was going to happen because when we arrived there was a group of boys standing around almost waiting for us. The boy we knew from school immediately walked up to me and threw a punch. I half slipped and it glanced off my cheek. But the fight had started. Despite how many altercations I've had, I remember very little of them, but I have very vivid memories of the brown handle and sharp blade of the knife the other boy pulled from his back pocket. He pointed the knife at me and gave me a choice: continue to fight and risk being stabbed or back down. At least I had a choice; when I was growing up it was still rare for knives to be used in street fights. Unfortunately, nowadays it's commonplace and often there is no warning. I've often thought that if I was a teenager today, or in the United States or Jamaica where the rate of violence is greater, with the target I seemingly had on my back, I probably wouldn't be alive. On that day, I immediately backed down. Outwardly I shrugged off the incident, but inwardly I was in pieces. Yet there was little I could do, so I put my feelings in a box and carried on. It was only when I was older that the box would be pried open and I would be forced to confront this and a host of other feelings.

Recognition has other consequences. If we attach reverence to the white coat of doctor, what do we attach to Black skin? It is this that partly explains why people show me their passes if I stand in the lobby of an office, thinking I'm the security officer, or why when entering a meeting people stay rooted to their chairs until they realize that I'm not bringing the tea or coffee. Yes, the Gavin Lewis you agreed to meet is in fact a Black man. But it also has consequences when we can't see ourselves represented in these companies and when the major route to these companies — education — is blocked.

Harvard psychologist Robert Rosenthal and elementary school principal Lenore Jacobson published *Pygmalion in the Classroom* (1968), describing a phenomenon called the

Pygmalion effect. The theory was named after the Greek myth of Pygmalion, a sculptor who fell in love with a statue he carved. In their book, Rosenthal and Jacobson argued there is a direct relationship between expectations and outcomes. In this, high expectations lead to better performance and low expectations lead to poor performance, and this is particularly prevalent in education. Although Black children had been given access to integrated schools following the passing of the US Civil Rights Act, their outcomes were vastly different from that of their White counterparts. The reasons behind this are complex and the persistent underperformance of Black children cannot be attributed to a single cause. Yet this idea of a self-fulfilling prophecy and the suggestion that schoolteachers could have lower expectations of their Black students and that this could be a factor in their underperformance was widely dismissed.

One of the attractions of the council estate we lived on were the local amenities. (The word "amenities" stems from the Latin word *amoenitas,* meaning pleasant.[14]) Next to one of the estate's many entrances was a row of shops, including a hairdresser, a launderette, and a grocery store. Across the road from the council estate was a school that the majority of kids from the estate and surrounding houses attended. This essentially meant that the residents need never leave the estate, which is fine until these amenities become unpleasant. I was one of many Black boys who attended this school, though when I look back it felt more like organized chaos, with schoolteachers more akin to prison wardens than figures employed to impart knowledge and guide children. I have distinct recollections of boredom; I would finish the work set by the teachers with ease but was never given any additional assignments. We were constantly spoken to harshly, admonished for any perceived infraction, and never given the benefit of the doubt. The environment was so unstimulating, but it also felt that my behavior as a result was what I should be doing, what was expected. There was no other way to be.

On one occasion when we were given a piece of work by the teacher, I was sitting next to a White girl who dove into the exercise with vigor. Competitive as ever, I also started the exercise in earnest, and we raced through the assignment to see who would finish first. She completed her work just before me and stuck her hand in the air to tell the teacher. I then finished and also put my hand in the air. The teacher came over and gleefully said, "Well done!" to the girl, but then looked across at me and asked how I had finished so quickly. I looked back at the teacher with confusion, but before I was able to say anything she said, "You know it's not good to copy other people's work." I protested but she shut down any discussion and walked away. Tears streamed down my cheeks, and I shouted out that I had completed the work myself. That was then enough to be reprimanded and sent out of the classroom for "insubordination." The next day I found that my seat had been moved next to another Black boy. It is only now that I realize that we were all sitting together at the back of the classroom along with the Black girls, where presumably we were easier to control and less likely to distract the White and Brown children.

So as I grew older, my mother grew increasingly concerned about my experience at school, and things came to head when a teacher attempted to stop a group of us running down the school corridor by grabbing my T-shirt, inflicting some deep scratches across my neck. My mum went to the school to establish why this had happened, but rather than discussing the incident, the teacher stated that she was concerned about my cognitive ability. According to her I had a temper and was presenting learning difficulties and perhaps should be referred to a "special school."

From the early 1960s to the early 1980s in England, hundreds of Black children were labeled as "educationally subnormal" (ESN), deemed to have low intelligence. These schools cemented the low expectations of these children and many left with barely any real qualifications and deep emotional and psychological wounds. In 1971, Grenadian politician Bernard Coard published *How the Caribbean Child Is Made Educationally Sub-normal in the British School System: The Scandal of the Black Child in Schools in Britain.* Coard had witnessed this trend first-hand and wrote the book to alert parents to the dangers of their children being labeled ESN. He promoted the book aggressively and gave talks around England to rooms full of parents. Caribbean parents at this time placed their faith in the school system; the idea of challenging it was anathema. Coard, however, asserted the practices of the schools of this time were racist and this permeated the curriculum itself. There was inadequate Black parental knowledge and involvement about what was happening to their children at school, the lack of a Black parental organization to mobilize action, and the need to establish supplementary schools, as well as low expectations of teachers and a commensurate poor self-image and poor self-esteem of Black children.

I was fortunate. My mother was attuned to these challenges and insisted that "Gavin is not of low intelligence." Others, friends of mine, were not so fortunate. Of those who found themselves in ESN schools, I know of one who is in prison, and one who is no longer alive. To give me a chance, my mother moved me out of the school in Tottenham and sent me to a school in a different borough. It was there that I would realize that being Black meant being different.

5

Zero-Sum Game

"OH, YOU NIGGER!" THE SCHOOL bus went silent. Tony slapped his hand over his mouth when he realized what he had just said. He looked at me and then at Brian, the only other Black boy on the bus. Everyone else looked at Tony and then at me and then at Brian. Tony and I were effectively best friends. We sat next to each other in class, departed school together, and he often waited until I boarded the bus back to Tottenham before he walked to his home in the then more affluent area of Enfield.

Then the questions came. "Gavin, Brian, are going to take that!?" "Are you going to beat Tony up!?" "You have to beat him up!"

Twice a week a bus came to collect all the students in our grade to take us to swimming lessons, about a 15-minute bus ride away. The school was tucked in a residential neighborhood, away from the busy main street. It always felt strange walking past rows of quiet front gardens, turning a corner, and seeing a large school emerge behind some intimidating wrought-iron fences. For the bus driver this presented a challenge; the narrow streets were not designed for a long, double-decker bus. The bus driver, Kenneth, greeted us with a sparkling smile as we boarded the bus. To turn the bus around after collecting the schoolchildren took some skill, and Kenneth would often have to shunt the bus backwards and forwards several times to reverse. The problem on this occasion was that someone had parked illegally near the school, so when Kenneth tried to turn the bus around, we got stuck. To free us would have meant hitting the car, driving into the railings, or reversing into one of the houses. Tony obviously wasn't impressed by this, so he shouted at Kenneth. We were on top deck, so Kenneth didn't hear; only Brian and I did.

The Latin term *niger* is an adjective describing the color black. In Spanish and Portuguese, the word evolved to became *negro,* while in English it became a noun to describe a Black person.[1] Some members of the Black community despise the word. But others in the community use it to greet or describe one another. I've been listening to hip-hop since the 1980s and have seen that US hip-hop and increasingly UK artists use the term freely, with the intent of taking the power out of it, effectively declaring that we don't own much but we can own this word and it remains off limits for you. I question how effective this has actually been. Once, as I boarded a train after work, I heard a group of young White women singing the word "nigger" with glee. They clammed up as soon as they saw me board, but for them the word wasn't off-limits; they took pleasure from it, but clearly knew the implications of using it. The fact that it is still regarded as the most hateful word you can use against a Black person demonstrates how much power it still has.

At the time Tony shouted this on the school bus, however, I had no idea what the term meant. I had never heard it before. The fact that Kenneth was Black and that the other kids on bus were asking if Brian and I would mete out justice as the only other Black people on the bus was lost on me. So as strange as it might sound, I realized I was Black, but I had no idea that I was *Black*.

━━━━━━

Overcoming socioeconomic disadvantage requires the creation of both social and economic advantage, which might mean an individual or segment of society begins to move through the established social hierarchy. This, however, is often met with resistance. This resistance can be covert, those subtle reasons for being overlooked or treated differently, where you know something is amiss but can't quite put your finger on it. It can be embedded in processes, procedures, and institutions. It can also be overt and even violent. There are many reasons for this resistance. It may be the result of an individual's beliefs or values in the existing social order. It may be a result of an individual's or group's own struggle for recognition. But it may also be the outcome of those who resist feeling they are disadvantaged and the gains of one group will result in further losses for them, a zero-sum game.

Game theory is a theoretical framework for conceiving social situations among competing players.[2] A zero-sum game is a situation in game theory in which one person's gain equals another person's loss.[3] Understanding and navigating this concept is critical to creating a viable solution to increasing both social and economic advantages for Black communities. Progressing socially or economically therefore means removing or overcoming barriers. Some are simply a by-product of a societal structure; others were created intentionally. This often becomes a double-edged sword. You might benefit from the advantages this affords, but it might mean disrupting the status quo. Because Black people often occupy the bottom rung of the socioeconomic hierarchy, those on the rung just above fear being thrown off as they clamber up.

Stella Dadzie is a British activist who founded the Organisation for Women of Asian and African Descent (OWAAD) in 1978.[4] She advocated for women's rights but against what she believed was a very White feminist movement. Dadzie and co-authors Beverly Bryan and Suzanne Scarf wrote *The Heart of Race* (1985), which addressed the experiences of Black British women. My mother attended a talk by Dadzie held in a community center in Tottenham. It was the first time she heard someone not only discussing a similar experience to hers but discussing how she could do more. Quite simply, my mother, like many other Black people, had no idea that she could aspire to achieve something, let alone how she might do this. Dadzie told a room full of Black women that they must set goals for themselves. "You are not just mothers and wives."

So my mother studied and passed the English tertiary qualification, O Level. Hearing a positive message can only do so much; experiences are what create real change. Achieving this qualification allowed my mother to believe she could also achieve and set another goal. She was introduced to a route into education called an access course that gave would-be students from lower-income households a free foundation qualification that would provide a path to university. I have vivid memories of my mother studying late into the night after giving my sister and me dinner. The decision to send me to a school outside of Tottenham was therefore driven by the need to give me a chance. She wanted to free me from the suffocating peer pressure that had reduced my world.

The atmosphere in the school I attended in Enfield was completely different from the school in Tottenham. The chaos that seemed to engulf me as soon as I approached the school gates was replaced with a calmness, almost a serenity, that was alien to me. No one cared about what I was wearing, no one challenged me to fight. My classmates seemed genuinely pleased to have someone new to talk to. The only thing that seemed to matter was whether I was any good at playing football and what team I supported. The schoolteachers seemed, well, normal, and for the first time I felt as if I was treated as a person with valuable thoughts, feelings, and opinions.

During a history class, the teacher, who was a White male called Mr. Brent, posed a question to the students. There were two or three bright students who were always the first the put their hands up. I felt I knew the answer but was incredibly reluctant to raise my hand, particularly in front of my new classmates. Mr. Brent scanned the classroom; he often picked on people who didn't put their hands up to answer. I had avoided this for the first few classes but I could feel the dread as his eyes settled on me. "Gavin?" I froze. "Would you like to answer?" Even though I was relatively sure of the subject matter, I was conditioned not to try. Failure was expected, so why bother? In a small voice I whispered an answer and waited for the inevitable. "Yes, that's right." Mr Brent then turned to the blackboard and wrote my answer up on the board. I was shocked, not only because I got the answer correct, but because Mr. Brent's voice, body language, and facial expressions didn't change. It was almost as if he expected me to provide the right answer. I glanced around and realized the other students, including the three who always responded first, were looking at me, not with cruel grins as I was marched to the headmaster's office after another fight, but with admiration.

Learning the history of Britain is important. It's the country I was born in and given the role it has played in world affairs for centuries, it's difficult to understand the world today without assessing the role Britain played. I do feel, however, there is a need to understand the history from a different perspective. Learning about the Kingdom of Kush, which ruled over a vast region of Africa what is now northern Sudan and southern Egypt from 1000 BCE to AD 350 would have told me that Black, or Nubian, people created complex societies and spawned a civilization that even ruled over the revered Egyptian empire. This history did not start with colonialism and that occupation did not civilize us. Rather, we created civilization. Emancipation from slavery was not just bestowed upon us by benevolent White liberals but Black people fought for it through the Great Jamaican Slave Revolt of 1831–32 or the German Coast Uprising of 1811, which inspired other revolts by the enslaved and struck fear into the hearts of White owners.

Today, there is a push to include Black history in school curriculum in some states in the US. In the UK, a movement called the Black Curriculum has been advocating for the incorporation of Black history into the UK national curriculum. I believe this would give Black students a sense of themselves and their history, and would also give White students an understanding of the history of their Black classmates.

But in addition to this we also need to ensure that young people are valued and their efforts are recognized. For as much as history has told us we are less, the day-to-day interactions of others are what affirms this view. It's the person who decides not to sit next to you on the bus. It's the security guard who follows you around the store. It's the boss who says you should be grateful. No matter how much I would have learned about my history, without being treated as an equal I wouldn't have believed I was. In Hegelian terms,

I was recognized by a teacher with no preconceptions and with the esteem my hard work afforded myself and others. I felt my lungs expand. My only sadness is that at the time, my mother felt I had to leave Tottenham to experience this. True change comes when all children can experience this regardless of their location or their access to education.

But for me to receive this benefit, I also experienced drawbacks. My presence was seen as a threat to those who either felt I didn't belong, or who became concerned about their own place in the world. For many groups wrestling with their own struggle for recognition, they would often turn not just on each other, but also us. To get to my new school I had to travel on a bus for about 40 minutes, which meant waking up earlier and arriving home later. The bus was often empty and I would have a whole section to myself. Every morning I would plant myself by the window and gaze at the changing landscape, from Tottenham's run-down council estates, betting shops, off-licenses, fast-food takeaways, and abandoned carpets rolled up to protect those sheltering from the rain, to Enfield's period houses, trees, and parks. The demographic also changed, from the predominately Black and Brown people of Tottenham to the predominately White people of Enfield. As I traveled away from Tottenham, I would feel myself relaxing, able to take in larger amounts of air. At first it felt like freedom. I didn't feel like a minority when I first began attending my new school; it was others who pointed out my differences.

A few months after the incident with Tony, I was walking from school to catch the bus home after a football match. Most of the other kids lived locally, so as usual I was walking by myself. Ahead of me was a mother, her two children, and another woman, whom I assumed to be a friend. The mother was pushing her youngest in a stroller while her older child walked alongside. I overtook the family; although it was summer and still light out, I was eager to get home. When I walked in front of the family, the child, who was probably a couple of years younger than me, pushed me in the back. I was surprised and looked at the kid and then the two women, but they just stared back at me. I sped up and the boy ran after me. He pushed me again and began to kick me from behind. I reacted and stepped on his toe. The mother then erupted, "How dare you touch my son!?" "He kicked me first!" I responded. "Where are you from!? Why don't you go back your own country!?" she asked. Confusion. In the moment I ran through all the plausible reasons why she would say this. "I was born here," I shouted to the woman. "You don't belong here, go back to your own country," she said. On the way home, the only answer I could of think was "London."

My mother was concerned about the racism I experienced but was equally encouraged about my progress, so she wanted me to attend a secondary school in Enfield. My primary school considered me to be a high-performing student and presented me with the opportunity to apply to a grammar school. These are schools free to attend but to achieve entry you have to take an exam. On the day of the exam there was some milling around and queueing among the other applicants. I was the only Black applicant in a sea of White students, but by now I was used to this.

What raised my blood pressure was the other students discussing how much they'd studied for the exam and how they had performed on the practice tests. By contrast I had simply turned up. I was very nervous when the proctor asked us to take our seats, and this only increased when I opened the booklet and read the first question, which asked us to state the next shape in a sequence of weird shapes. I'm sure some kids are so bright they would pass such an exam without preparation, but the majority need to prepare, through access to practice exams and expensive tutors. My primary school was good, but they left such decisions to the kids and their families. Middle-class parents are aware of how to navigate the system. They may have been through the same process themselves or have friends, family, or colleagues to guide them. A single-parent family in living Tottenham often does not. More damaging, however, is the narrative: you are told that only the brightest kids get into the school. At the time I felt there was a tier of ability and I wasn't as clever as the other kids. It's a message that still permeates today, when in fact the real determinant is access and aspiration.

So rather than attending a grammar school, I was left with the schools in Enfield that would accept a child who had no entrance exam and had space for a child who didn't live locally. Unsurprisingly, these schools were in less demand and deemed to have lower standards of teaching. I'm not sure this is actually the case; it's more that they drew in students with more challenging socioeconomic backgrounds, and the key was achieving the national average. The school I was accepted into struggled, but my mother felt this would still give me a better chance.

Off I went again, but this school was much deeper into Enfield on the borders of Hertfordshire, where there were even fewer Black people. I wasn't the only Black pupil in the school; a few other parents in Tottenham also sent their children out of the borough in the belief this would give them a better chance. But we were the first to ever attend and the local racist gang whose brothers and sisters attended the school were not impressed. "Nigger's out" was permanently graffitied on the side of a building near the school, so every morning when the bus we traveled on climbed to the top of the hill, we were greeted with these words.

Interestingly the word of choice of wasn't nigger but "coon," a shortened form of racoon derived from a caricature of Black people from the Jim Crow era. There were two caricatures used to depict Black people. The first was Sambo, who was portrayed as childlike, lazy, and easily frightened, but also as a loyal servant. The character was often used as a justification for slavery. How could it be wrong when these dumb creatures wanted and almost needed servitude? The coon character, however, was portrayed as older; although he was still childlike, he did not accept his position in servitude. He was just too lazy to do anything about it. This became the preeminent but also most damaging stereotype: Black people who were considered too lazy to change their position and would rather eat watermelons and steal chickens.[5]

The first time I heard the term it was inflicted on a friend at school. He was having an animated conversation with a White girl who casually said, "You silly coon," in front of a large group of people. No one reacted. Again, I had no idea what the term meant but knew enough by then that it was a racial insult. I do sometimes wonder how racists select their words. Do they research the meaning of each one and decide which is most applicable? Or maybe it's decided by the day of the week: nigger on Monday, coon on Tuesday. . . . But as well as inflicting harm, it's also an attempt to maintain the social hierarchy, positioning us as less and, consequently, them as more. These verbal insults became normal, but as we got older and turned from boys to young men, we were seen as more of a threat. To maintain the status quo, words turned to violence.

I was 15 years old when Stephen Lawrence was murdered. Stephen was a Black teenager killed while he and his friend Duwayne Brooks were waiting for a bus in Eltham in southeast London, which was about a 20-minute bus ride from Stephen's home in Plumstead. It was 10 p.m. and Stephen and Duwayne had visited an uncle of Stephen's to play video games, but they missed the last bus on their usual route home. They decided to take a different route and at 10:25 p.m.

Stephen walked a few meters along the road to see if he could see a bus coming. Duwayne was still at the bus stop when five White youths emerged and approached Stephen. Duwayne heard them shouting, "What, what nigger?" before surrounding Stephen and stabbing him five times in the shoulder and collarbone, which severed his auxiliary arteries and punctured his lung. Stephen lost all feeling in his right arm as his attackers fled. Duwayne ran to escape with Stephen staggering behind him. Stephen soon collapsed and bled to death and was pronounced dead on his arrival at Brook General Hospital at 11:05 p.m. on April 22, 1993.[6]

After Stephen's murder, things got worse. Stephen looked like us and was attacked and killed by a White gang. We traveled to their heartland every day. If one of us had detention, a football match, or basketball game, the rest of us had to hang around to accompany him home. Being alone after dark at school with the gang lurking was a no-no. The White gang became brazen, walking through the school calling us coons and niggers. Worse was that some of their siblings at the school—some younger than us—would call us racist slurs knowing they were protected by their brothers and cousins, who were older and feared. One evening after a school disco, two of the siblings decided to "beat up some niggers." I remember it was a summer and still light and we were slowly walking to the bus stop for the long journey home. Some of the older pupils were with us but they seemed to be keeping to themselves, so we let our guard down. I was laughing at a joke and turned round when—smack!—the whole world seemed to light up with stars and flashes. I had been punched square in the nose, which erupted with blood. The other Black kids saw what happened; some were sympathetic, others angry. I tried to pretend that it wasn't a big deal and would enact revenge when the opportunity arose. The reality was that I was devastated.

One aspect I didn't expect as I progressed at school was that those who I previously identified with would also become a barrier. A few months after the disco event, I was traveling home from school, watching the number of trees decline to be replaced by boarded-up shop fronts. Because I attended a different school, my uniform was different. I had never considered this an issue until a group of boys from another school in Edmonton, an area just outside of Tottenham, boarded the bus. They didn't recognize my uniform and immediately questioned where I was from. I was sitting on the deck toward the back and aside from a couple of people seated in the front, the bus was empty. I knew something was about to happen as they spied me before they got on; I had seen them talking and looking at me before boarding. There were three of them; one sat behind me, another to the side, and one at the front. They were older than me and wore their trousers halfway down their waists—at the time we called then "rude boys"—and they all wore bright white Nike Air Max shoes. "Where are you from!?" a smaller boy demanded to know. Before I could answer, the boy next to me said, "He goes to a pussy school." They paused to see how I would react, a test. Saying something would have escalated things further; saying nothing implied that I accepted what they said.

I felt the familiar butterflies in my stomach, the adrenaline rushing through me to prepare me for an altercation. I had been in enough fights by that point to know where this was heading. These situations are in part the continued struggle for recognition. But they are also a symptom of deprivation within the same communities, the idea that one's progress is detrimental to another's. We can trace this back to the divide-and-conquer legacy of slavery. But other deprived races also face this challenge, locked in their own zero-sum game. This barrier was also erected by the institutions designed to protect us. I made a snap decision and jumped out of my seat, over the seat in front of me, kicking the boy in front, which stunned him. I almost fell down the stairs and burst through the passengers who had just boarded and through the closing doors. I didn't stop to look behind me and ran down the street. I ran so hard and for so long that my legs went numb. All I could feel was my heart, until that's all I was, a heart running.

The feeling in my legs began to return when I saw two uniformed men standing by a car with blue lights flashing. Upon seeing me running they started to walk toward me. I thought, "Ah, I'm safe," but one of the men pulled his radio to his mouth while the other shouted, "Stop!" and "We've got you." Their interpretation of social order was that a Black boy running meant he was up to no good. I wanted to explain what had happened but remembered one of the unwritten rules: don't talk to the police. Years of mistrust had been translated to a street code that prevented me from saying what I was feeling, which was that I was scared. Instead, I said nothing, and the men then stood on either side of me, while one asked me to empty my pockets and searched my bag. He then asked me, "So where are you from?"

Stephen Lawrence's murder become front-page news. It went unsolved until a right-wing newspaper, the *Daily Mail*, led a campaign to have the White perpetrators who had been tried but acquitted retried until they were finally imprisoned in 2012. A review was also held into the UK's Metropolitan Police's handling of Stephen's murder on orders of the then–Home Secretary Jack Straw and led by Sir William Macpherson, a high court judge. The report found that the Metropolitan Police's approach to Stephen's murder was a principal reason the Lawrence family had to wait nearly 20 years for justice, labeling the force "institutionally racist." By definition, marginalized groups struggle to remove these barriers, so they are left with little choice but to protest. This might lead to reform, but without real change we are forever locked in a cycle of atrocity, protest, and further reform—until another atrocity occurs.

Broadwater Farm, or "the Farm," is a council estate built in the 1960s that offered affordable housing to poor White and Black residents. The 1980s saw a series of riots, the most serious occurring in Brixton, London; Toxteth, Liverpool; Handsworth, Birmingham; and Chapeltown, Leeds. They were all carried out by majority Black communities. The Brixton riots were sparked by the accidental shooting of Dorothy "Cherry" Groce during a police search. She was left paralyzed during the incident when the police were in search of her son. The following week, on October 5, 1985, Cynthia Jarrett, a Broadwater Farm resident, died of a heart attack when the police entered her home in search of stolen property after the arrest of her son Floyd. No stolen goods were found. On October 6, a peaceful protest led by Cynthia's relatives outside Tottenham police station saw tensions rise as police attempts to disperse the crowd were met with resistance. The discontent spread, as police entered Mount Pleasant Road, The Avenue, and Willan Road, which led to Broadwater Farm, and were pelted with bottles and debris, and buildings and cars were set alight. PC Keith Blakelock, who was assisting in the protection of the firemen who were attempting to put out a blaze, was surrounded and set upon by a group of youths. He died of multiple knife wounds.[7]

I was eight years old at the time so I don't remember much about the riots, but my mother recalls them vividly. She watched events unfold on our color television. Like most people in the UK at the time, she had seen footage of the riots in other parts of the country, but this was in Tottenham—much closer to home. She understood why riots erupted; there is only so much oppression and persecution a group can take before they react. Her view is that Black people in Tottenham at that time did not have the means to express their discontent about their socioeconomic situation and, more pointedly, methods of policing. Today the Broadwater Farm riots are remembered for the murder of PC Keith Blakelock and for the imprisonment of the "Tottenham three": Winston Silcott, Engin Raghip, and Mark Braithwaite.[8] Such was the pressure to make an arrest that a whole host of errors was made during the investigation, including false statements, tampering with evidence, and coercion.

Attempts to protest through the courts rarely gained traction. The authorities viewed their Black residents as "troublesome" and needing to be contained. The whole situation was a tinderbox waiting for a spark to set it alight. But my mother also expressed dismay that this was the only way we could draw attention to the underlying issues. Today, in the 30 years since the riots, she questions whether anything really changed.

In Los Angeles on March 3, 1991, Rodney Glen King was beaten by LAPD officers during his arrest for driving while intoxicated. The brutal beating was captured on film and sent to a local news station. Footage of King lying on the ground was beamed around the world and caused a public outrage. Four police officers were tried on charges of excessive force; however, three were acquitted and the jury failed to reach a verdict on the fourth. This sparked six days of rioting in Los Angeles in 1992, until the National Guard was called in to quell the unrest. The federal government did convict two of the officers in 1993 for violation of King's civil rights. The Christopher Commission, ordered by then-mayor Tom Bradley, undertook a full examination of the police department's structure and operations following the riots and its findings focused on the force's default use of excessive force and the failure of management to prevent this.[9]

These atrocities became the face of racism, which is problematic because racism isn't always violent. It can be an act, a belief, or an attitude. Following the conviction of the Rodney King officers and Stephen Lawrence's murderers, the UK and US seemingly moved to a post-racial society, where racism was deemed a thing of the past. Why? Because when the White majority pick up a newspaper or switch on the news, they weren't confronted with the specter of a Black person dying or being beaten at the hands of a White person. Government policy only served to affirm this view. In the UK, this took the form of multiculturalism. Under the Labour Government of Tony Blair, a policy adopted that celebrated the different ethnic makeup of the UK. Against a backdrop of economic growth, it advocated for minority cultures to remain distinct from the dominant culture of the UK. Critics of multiculturalism argue this created greater divisions in society. It effectively stopped the integration of minority groups and prevented the dominant White Britons from recognizing their own cultural identity. Regardless of its intention, what this policy did prevent is a discourse about race in the UK, effectively putting a lid on those who claimed to experience racism and preventing the White majority who also felt disenfranchisement from being heard.

This post-racial era also prevented an understanding of the intersection between race, society, and economics. The approach is too often to criminalize entire segments of society, without ever getting to the root causes of the issue, which are social and economic in nature. The 1994 the US Crime Bill, which was overseen by Senator Joe Biden under Bill Clinton's presidency, imposed tougher prison sentences at the federal level and encouraged states to do the same. It provided funds for states to build more prisons, funded 100,000 more police officers, and supported grant programs that encouraged police to carry out more drug-related arrests. This was designed to be a tough-on-crime approach that would be beneficial for wider society. This focus on drug arrests was a particular problem when combined with the Anti-Drug Abuse Act of 1986. This created significant disparities in sentencing between crack and powdered cocaine. Under the bill, a person was sentenced to a five year-prison sentence for possession of just 5 grams of crack cocaine, but it took possession of 500 grams of powdered cocaine to receive the same sentence. Crack is a cheaper alternative to powdered cocaine and as a result is more prominent in low-income neighborhoods, which were more likely to be Black. Consequently, Black communities suffered greatly from a crack cocaine epidemic, from the effects of policing, and from mass incarceration, which only served to exacerbate, not solve, the underlying challenges US Black communities faced.[10]

Many of the poor White people I attended school with also lived in single-parent families with low incomes. One fellow pupil, a White guy called Daniel, had become a close friend. He was a talented footballer and would often jump on the bus for a couple of stops with us to head home to his mum. Around the age of 14, Daniel dropped out of school and began hanging around the local racist gang. It was a very weird feeling; he was still our friend yet began to hate us because we were Black. He saw no future in education, yielded to peer pressure, and joined a gang, an all too familiar story. The difference was that rather than attacking each other, they believed they had found a common enemy in Black people. I initially struggled with this because I couldn't help but notice the similarities. If those on the next rung of the ladder were able to look up, would there be less resistance to us?

Perhaps finding a solution to create socioeconomic progression of Black communities could be used to remove barriers to their progression by helping other demographics. It may manifest itself differently within certain communities and it's important not to dilute the unique experience of Black people with the experience of White people, but there is a common denominator and that is inequality. Black people in the US and UK, poor White people in the US, White working-class people in the UK, Native Americans, Australian Aborigines, and North Africans in France are all impacted negatively by inequality.

But there is one stark difference between White and Black communities and that is the threat many White communities feel. According to the 2020 US Census, the United States is 57.8% White, 18.7% Hispanic, 12.4% Black, and 6% Asian. The White population has declined by 8.6% since 2010, while the multiracial population, defined as being of two or more races, has seen a 276% increase since 2010.[11] The diversification of the United States shows no sign of abating. Yet how do you put this on the agenda? How do you campaign and force change when your priority is simply feeding and clothing yourself? Only when the situation becomes acute do the communities vent their frustration through what feels like the only method available: protest. And to prevent the cycle of atrocity, protest, and reform, we need real change that tackles social and economic disadvantage and a framework for measuring and implementing this in an increasingly diverse society, in our institutions, and in ourselves. Perhaps then we will understand that Black progression is actually a win-win and is beneficial for all.

6

Almonds

THERE ARE MANY SYMPTOMS OF socioeconomic disadvantage. The tendency is to focus on these rather than on the root cause. One of these symptoms is the treatment of Black people who find themselves requiring mental health services. This adversely impacts Black communities, and attempts to treat this need to be accelerated. But if we fail to resolve the negative experiences that lead to mental health challenges, it will continue to be an issue for many.

When people learn about my background and then my role in finance, they often ask me: What made you different? Certainly my mother played a pivotal role in my life. But it's a question I've never quite known how to answer. Achieving success in any field also brings with it the danger that you can begin to feel you are different, almost special. I've met many who have achieved amazing things, against the odds, but who have become arrogant. It also creates the impression that there is some hidden, innate quality that only a few people have. For the elite athlete or inspiring musician, perhaps this is true. But the corporate world is full of hardworking and competent people who simply attended the right school or were given the right advice. If we bestow some secret gift on those who didn't have these advantages yet managed to break into the world, then success is forever out of reach for the vast majority of people. And yet I must recognize that it is uncommon for someone with my background to hold a senior position in finance. So I usually shrug my shoulders and say, "I'm not sure." But if I were to provide an honest response, I would say, "Almonds."

The amygdala is a small cluster of almond-shaped cells located near the base of the brain. We all have two of these groups, one in each hemisphere of our brain. The role of the amygdala is to regulate emotions such as joy, sadness, and happiness. It also preserves memories and attaches emotions to these memories, known as emotional remembrances. So we not only remember an interaction with a loved one but feel the emotion we attribute to that loved when recollecting them.[1] The amygdala also plays an important role in activating the flight-or-fight response. When we feel we are in danger or facing a threat, the brain signals stress hormones to be released, which prepares the body to either flee or fight for survival. (There is a dog growling angrily at me. Do I run or prepare to fend it off?)

In another part of the brain are the frontal lobes, which are part of the cerebral cortex. The cerebral cortex regulates voluntary actions such as reasoning, movement, and decision-making. The frontal lobes have an important relationship with the amygdala because they allow us to evaluate our emotions and respond accordingly. (I see that although the dog is angry, it's on a leash and therefore my response is to walk away.) Both of these functions are vital to our survival and played a role in human evolution. When we were walking the plains, the risk of attack from an animal or another tribe was high, so we had to be on constant alert.[2]

In relation to the amygdala nowadays, the medical and physiological communities usually state something along the lines of, *Today the pressures of modern life can trigger our stress responses at work or in relationships.* But for deprived communities, that stress is often greater and starts from a much earlier age. It also stems from factors such as the struggle to meet basic needs like food or shelter and being constantly on alert for violence or the threat of it.

One guy I lived near was Jamal. He was tall, a talented athlete, popular with girls, the type of person who was revered, plus he had an older brother who gave him instant street credibility. He liked to smoke weed, which wasn't uncommon. Many might think this is typical of Black people—another stereotype—but in my experience the White people I attended university with and worked with smoked just as much and actually partook of much harder drugs. Jamal, however, began to smoke a lot. At first it was just occasional, but after his older brother was tragically stabbed to death, we noticed he started to smoke more and more, to the point where a visit to his house meant we would be greeted with plumes of smoke and his bloodshot eyes. I lost contact with Jamal over the years but heard through the grapevine that he was having a hard time.

A few years after I had graduated from university, I was working in my first job. I was on my way home and waiting to board a bus. A disheveled man approached me from behind. I spun round, and he said, "Gavin," then shuffled away. I was baffled as I got on the bus. I sat down and looked out of the window and saw that he was now on the other side of the road looking at me. Then it dawned on me: Jamal. He had matted dreadlocks, missing teeth, and was dressed in rags. Whether this was a reaction to smoking, whether he moved onto other substances, or whether something else happened, I'm not sure. But he wasn't the guy I once knew. You might think this is an extreme example, but I can count at least five other guys I grew up with who are now in a similar place. What links them all is an aversion to their reality, the same reality I also wanted to get away from.

When thinking about crime in the Black community, the focus is typically on Black people as perpetrators. A common stereotype is that Black men are thieves or robbers. We never discuss the fact that in the UK between April 2017 and March 2020, Black men and men from mixed ethnic backgrounds were 21% more likely to be victims of crime than men from any other ethnic group.[3] During the COVID-19 pandemic, the homicide rate increased from 5.8 per 100,000 Americans in 2019 to 7.5 per 100,000 in 2020. Black Americans account for 13.5% of the US population but during the pandemic the homicide rate for Black Americans rose from 22.9% per 100,000 in 2019 to 30.7% in 2020. For all other Americans, the rate went from 3.2 to 3.8%.[4] Clearly there is a physical consequence to this, but I'm not sure we've even begun to comprehend the emotional aspect.

I can recall the majority of the violent incidents in my life. Although they live long in my memory, these moments were actually short-lived—a fight that felt like it lasted for hours was actually a few minutes. But there is also an aspect we don't actually recall: the threat or possibility that something might happen. The body is an amazing machine. When you are faced with danger, the amygdala sends a distress signal; another part of the brain, the hypothalamus, activates the sympathetic nervous system by sending signals through the autonomic nerves to the adrenal glands. These glands respond by pumping the hormones epinephrine, more commonly called adrenaline, and cortisol, the body's stress hormone, into your bloodstream. This process allows the body to pump more oxygen into the muscles. Your pain receptors are numbed, and the body is prepared to fight. This is why my voice always warbled when I was in a fraught situation and why my right leg always shook. I always mistook it for fear, but it was actually my body preparing itself to fight. This state is short-lived; the body simply cannot maintain this state for long periods of time. Yet, if the threat of violence is ever present, we can enter a low-grade state of readiness that has long-term implications. If cortisol levels remain elevated, a range of health problems can occur, including headaches, heart disease, weight gain, and insomnia.[5]

Without access to counseling, Jamal dealt with his grief and numbed the pain by seeking refuge in substances. Counseling would of course help, but the real answer here is to reduce the death rate of young Black men, and that means improving their life outcomes. I wanted to escape my environment through education while learning how to protect myself.

I attended my first boxing lesson at age 15, in a sweaty gym in Tottenham with taped-up punching bags attached to the ceiling with rusty chains that screeched with pain at each swing. The coach was an older guy who had boxed at both professional and amateur levels. To say he was unwelcoming is putting it mildly. Most of his attention was focused on his prospects, the boys who showed real promise; everyone else was essentially fodder. During my second or third lesson, I was called away from my footwork and bag drills and into the gym to do some "light sparring." A foul-smelling head-guard with peeling leather was thrown at me. "Glasses off," the coach said. This was problem for me because I was really near-sighted. I put on the headguard, squinted to improve my blurred vision, and tentatively held up my hands. Opposite me in the ring was another boy. We were probably around the same age, but he bounced around on his toes and shad-owboxed, whereas I stood flat-footed, rooted to the spot. I didn't even see the punches coming; I took one to the ribs and then a flurry more that had me curled up in the corner.

The coach called time before the bell even rang and, in disgust, told me to get out.

This was chastening. I really felt the need to learn how to fight, but the process felt almost the same as the fighting itself. I would get incredibly nervous the day before I attended a class. When I entered the gym, a now familiar feeling of butterflies in my stomach took over as my brain signaled to my body to get ready to fight. But these lessons were something I felt I needed to do, to protect myself, to stop being vulnerable, maybe to find a way to let go of a handful of almonds.

After routinely getting worked over in the gym and having a constant headache, I thought I would try something different. I took a look in the business directory (this was before the age of the internet) and found a school advertising "Chinese Boxing." I gave them a call and a friendly male voice answered. The first question I asked was whether wearing glasses was problem. He reassuringly said, "Glasses are no problem at all," and that the beginners' classes were Tuesday and Thursday evenings. Chinese boxing, or Wing Chun, is very different from Western boxing, more traditional, requiring a kung-fu uniform and slippers. with a grading system and different ranks as you progressed.

The training was really tough, and I loved it. Twice a week we would train for two hours. Wing Chun is fast paced, with fighting at very close quarters. There are kicks in the system but the majority of the action is standing up and focused on the hands. I would arrive at each lesson tense with anticipation and would leave dripping in sweat. I think it was the fact that it was so hard that attracted me to Wing Chun. I progressed quickly through the ranks; a mixture of athletic ability and too many fights in the playground had given me an aptitude for the art. For most people this would be enough, but becoming proficient was less about the art itself and more about surviving a street fight. This was despite the fact that as I got older, I was becoming less likely to be targeted. Nevertheless, I was preoccupied with how able I was to defend myself and began to research what other attributes I needed to equip myself with. I began to add in different fighting styles: Muay Thai, street fighting with knives, bottles, back to boxing, and eventually grappling.

Brazilian Jiu-Jitsu is a ground-based system, and I began to study it because, although I had spent years striking, I worried about what would happen if the fight hit the floor. Punching and kicking aren't nearly as effective if you're lying on your back. BJJ, as it's often referred to, was created in 1920 by the legendary Gracie family, who adapted a Japanese style of judo introduced to them by a Judoka called Mitsuyo Maeda. It's an amazing system, utilizing holds, chokes, and throws to defeat your opponent. It was designed for smaller opponents to defeat larger opponents. Although strength, stamina, and flexibility are important, it is more reliant on technique and leverage than on force. By the time I began practicing BJJ, I had already been training for around 10 years. This was in addition to lifting weights for strength, running for endurance, and yoga for flexibility.

My first grappling class was so strange. The grapplers wore a traditional uniform called a gi, yet they were covered in sometimes elaborate patches and there was music blasting through a set of loudspeakers. The techniques taught were alien to me; I had never grappled before. But the real magic was in live sparring, or "rolling," where you were able to practice in a live environment. If my previous fighting experience was tough, this was on a different level. I was manhandled by a guy half my size, who barely broke a sweat. If you get caught in a choke or a lock, you have to submit by tapping the mat or your opponent. This has happened so many times during my BJJ journey, it no longer bothers me. But when I first started grappling, it was a huge blow to my fragile ego. There is something about "giving up" that I just couldn't get used to.

BJJ is an arduous martial art. It takes an average of 10 years to reach the rank of black belt and the majority of practitioners never make it. I trained up to five times a week, competing in tournaments, all while working in the finance industry and raising a family. I even ran a school that at its height had over 50 students. I'm immensely proud of this. I've learned so much about myself and other people and its enabled me to stay in great condition. Yet the journey has taken its toll: countless injuries, extreme tiredness, and less time with my family. By the time I achieved my black belt, I was no longer in danger. My life had changed completely.

It's this same drive that focused my attention on education. For me, education was initially an escape route. In the UK, there were two key exams: GCSEs at age 16 and A Levels at age 18. During my GSCEs, I was still subject to the peer pressure that holds back so many Black boys. I fell out with a group of friends and became distracted just when I was sitting my exams. Despite this, I still achieved excellent grades. It wasn't long before I realized that I'm probably wired differently and maybe I should embrace this difference. So, when I began studying for my A Levels, it felt like life or death: either achieve a good education and change my life or stay in a world in which I didn't belong. Attending university and learning to defend myself physically quite literally became my dual sole focus, almost my reason for being.

My A Level grades were excellent and my teachers encouraged me to apply to Oxford or Cambridge. However, the thought of attending university and returning to London as "posh" made me feel I would become an even bigger target. With the added burden of racking up student debt, I dismissed the idea of Oxford and Cambridge completely. I still attended a prestigious university; however, this was in the safety of London, where I could live at home. My experience was therefore completely different from that of my White peers who had moved out of the home to stay on campus. So while they partied on the weekend and completed essays at the last minute, I worked in a supermarket and completed every assignment as if my life depended on it.

It is tempting to view martial arts and a focus on education as if they were positives, but they are still symptoms. Many people tell me that if it weren't for these experiences, I wouldn't be where I am now. I agree that facing challenges in life builds resilience and develops attributes that can enable success in life. One of my closest friends, Trevor, and I used to describe every year as a boxing match, with the 12 months of the year equivalent to 12 rounds. It always felt like a fight. But I do not believe trauma is healthy.

I first began to wonder if I had a problem after completing my degree. It had been a huge effort and I always felt that if I achieved the qualification, then a huge weight would be off my shoulders. But after finishing my secondary school studies, receiving my grades, and having the choice of universities, I couldn't relax. I thought this might be the stress of the last year, which was particularly intense. Even after a long break, I was still stuck in survival mode. Without the goal of university to channel this energy, I began to worry about a host of other things. The guy I had a beef with years ago. My health. The decision I had made about university. It might have been normal to worry about these things, but even after rationalizing them I just couldn't turn the worry off. My girlfriend at the time witnessed this first-hand and suggested I talk to someone.

There are certain moments in life that upon reflection change your course. The simple act of seeking professional help stopped me from spiraling. Yet too many others get caught in the maelstrom and never pull themselves out. If you have witnessed or experienced violence, there is a high probability that you are traumatized. If you have an absent parent, there is a high probability that you are traumatized. If you constantly worry about having enough money, there is a high probability that you are traumatized. Trauma manifests in many different ways; a short-term reaction can be shock, but longer-term reactions, particularly if perception of the threat remains, manifest as numbness as a way to cope. It might feel that you are handling the situation, but the trauma often finds a way to express itself through physical symptoms, such as digestive issues or headaches, and emotionally through depression, anxiety, or, in my case, post-traumatic stress disorder.

Recognizing and labeling my own experience was a watershed moment. Diagnosing the issue allowed me to begin to recover. This has been a long and difficult journey. Having that handful of almonds in my brain enabled me to change my life but I also realized that at some point this is a huge burden because it also reinforces the feeling of vulnerability. Undertaking cognitive behavioral therapy enabled me to manage and order my symptoms. My therapist was incredibly empathetic, and just having a person who didn't judge me was a relief.

After a few years I felt I really needed to understand not only where my drive was coming from but also my fear, so I did some research and found schema therapy. This enabled me to realize that my childhood experiences shaped the way I see the world. This realization allowed me to begin to heal emotionally. Despite this I was still prone to the odd bout of anxiety. Therapists often told me I would always suffer from this, but I refused to believe that I couldn't heal more. I then tried hypnotherapy, which targeted my subconscious thoughts. It was very effective, perhaps because I had invested so much in healing already; maybe it wouldn't have been so effective on its own. Nevertheless, this step really allowed me to open my hand and let the metaphorical almonds fall to the floor.

This journey has also enabled me to reflect on the wider implications. Firstly, mental health is relevant to everyone, but it's particularly important for men to recognize this. Part of the healing process is to voice and discuss how you feel. If I can generalize for a moment, women find this easier to do than men. Masculinity essentially means being strong, tough, able. Discussing feelings is often seen a weakness. It's no wonder why the biggest killer of men under the age of 45 is suicide. I have met some incredibly strong people; many have been street tough, others have made the sports or corporate world their domain. But the one thing they have in common is a mental health issue. There is a stigma among men in discussing this subject; there is an even greater stigma amongst Black men. Some rappers have tackled the subject. UK rapper Stormzy has openly discussed his battle with depression and urged his fans to stop smoking weed. On his 2017 track "Lay Me Bare," he wrote:

Like man, I get low sometimes, so low sometimes
Airplane mode on my phone sometimes
Sitting in my house with tears on my face
Can't answer the door to my bro sometimes

But we need to have a greater discourse about the issue.

I have known two individuals who have died by suicide. One of these was a White man who held a senior position in a bank. From the outside at least, he appeared to have it all together: a house, a family, children. Yet despite this he felt he couldn't go on, and ended his life in his mid-40s. Another was a promising athlete of mixed heritage. He was popular, incredibly personable, and had a bright future ahead of him. But he couldn't see it, or didn't feel he did, and ended his own life in his early 20s. When we look at the figures for Black men, it's frightening. A study published in June 2021 in the *Journal of the American Medical Association* revealed that between 1991 and 2017 Black male adolescents represented the largest increase in suicide attempts of any group, at 162.4%.

Age is also a factor. Trauma experienced at an early age can shape the way individuals see the world, with the impact lasting long into adulthood. Yet Black children are experiencing so much that many are impacted before they even get to adulthood. A study by the US Nationwide Children's Hospital in 2018 showed that Black children aged 5 to 12 were twice as likely to die from suicide as their White counterparts. Newer areas of research even suggest that trauma can be passed down through generations. Intergenerational trauma is the theory that trauma can be inherited because there is genetic change in a person's DNA. The changes from trauma do not damage the gene, resulting in genetic change; instead, it alters how a gene functions, known as epigenetic change. For example, in 2008 researchers found an association between prenatal exposure to famine and the risk of disease of the person in later life. More conclusive research may be required, but it raises the prospect that the trauma faced by our parents, grandparents, and great-grandparents may have been handed down to us, in addition to the challenges we still face today.[6]

Cognitive behavioral therapy is now available for NHS patients in the UK, and Obamacare and most other health insurance plans have provided most US citizens with access to counseling and therapy. But access to treatment is not enough; we also have to confront bias in healthcare. I think about Jamal and how he ended up in his situation. Maybe he did seek help but was misdiagnosed? Black men in the US and UK are more likely to be misdiagnosed with schizophrenia, even though they display symptoms typical of patients with depression. A study published in *Psychiatric Services* in February 2019 examined the medical records of 1,657 people at a community behavioral health clinic that included screening new patients for major depression as part of its assessment for schizophrenia. The study, which included 599 Black patients and 1,058 non-Latino White patients, found that clinicians failed to effectively weigh mood symptoms when diagnosing schizophrenia among Black patients, which suggests the presence of racial bias in diagnosing patients, whether conscious or subconscious. Factors such as epigenetics, discrimination, and even diet can all play a role. Michael Gara, a professor of psychiatry at the Robert Wood Johnson Medical School at Rutgers University, concluded that there has been a tendency for clinicians to overemphasize the relevance of psychotic symptoms and overlook symptoms of major depression in African Americans compared with other racial or ethnic groups. No studies show that African Americans with schizophrenia are more likely to also have major depression.

But again, the real solution is to reduce Black communities' exposure to traumatic experiences

We first need to understand that there is a link between social challenges such as poverty and life outcomes. In 2018, the *Metro* newspaper published two maps highlighting the most deprived areas of London and another map showing crime hotspots. The overlap was stark, with only some neighboring boroughs showing comparable rates of crime to the deprived boroughs because the deprived were traveling to more affluent areas to commit crimes. Reducing poverty has to be an imperative.

We also need to change the way we tackle these symptoms. Established in 2005, Scotland's Violence Reduction Unit

(VRU) approached knife and gun crime not just as a policing issue but as a public health issue. In 2004 and 2005, there were 137 homicides in Scotland, with 40 in Glasgow alone. By 2016 and 2017, the number had reduced to 62.[7] The program focused on five key areas: 1) reducing the influence of gangs through a no-tolerance, approach along with outreach by community leaders and former gang members; 2) offering vulnerable young people alternatives such as youth clubs; 3) drafting medical professionals to discuss the impact of knife and gun crimes in schools; 4) reducing the number of exclusions and placing a greater emphasis on education; and 5) finding routes to employment for young people so they have something to aspire toward.[8]

Similarly Black women are two to six times more likely to suffer maternal death than White women.[9] Social factors play a role, such as low income or education, food insecurity, and exposure to trauma. Many women then wrestle with postnatal or postpartum depression, which occurs during pregnancy or after birth. But crucially, biases in diagnosing the health symptoms increase this risk. For example, doctors' perception of Black women's ability to withstand pain also mean they are less likely to receive adequate pain relief or medication.

And finally, we need to assess the economic impact. An estimated 1 billion people worldwide suffer from a mental disorder.[10] Lost productivity resulting from the two most common mental disorders, depression and anxiety, cost the global economy USD$1 trillion each year. This is estimated to reach $6 trillion a year by 2030.[11] The lifetime costs of perinatal depression and anxiety alone to mother and child have been estimated between $112,299 and $51,622, respectively.[12] But despite these startling figures, the 2017 WHO Mental Health Atlas found that expenditure on mental health accounted for less than 2% of government health budgets.

And yet the economic case is compelling. For every $1 invested in scaled-up treatment for depression and anxiety, there is a $4 return in better health and productivity.[13] Programs aimed at intervening with at-risk children in the United States have shown a net positive outcome. These ranged between $1.80 and $3.30 for every $1 spent on programs targeted at children with behavioral problems.[14]

Achieving this requires a different approach, one that combines social considerations with economic outcomes. One-off interventions simply do not go far enough. The approach needs to intervene during an individual's journey through life, what we call their lifecycle. It requires a joined-up approach between governments, grassroots organizations, and the private sector, and must address issues spanning mental and physical health, education, employment, and access to finance. The Lancet Commission on report global mental health and sustainable development, published in 2018, called for a partnership between academic institutions, UN agencies, development banks, grassroots organizations, and the private sector to mobilize and invest in funds to transform mental health. If we can establish a framework for resolving inequality, this can be applied to the unique experience different demographics face.

We should also think about the potential contributions of Black people to the economy. We should seek to reduce inequality but also need to be realistic that disadvantaged communities will probably have to work harder to achieve the same results as those who have greater advantage. To navigate this environment requires a host of attributes, including resilience, conceptual thinking, work ethic, and adaptability. In an increasingly uncertain and changing world, corporations should be scrambling to acquire individuals with these skill sets. If we can begin to quantify the contribution, then the case for investing becomes even more urgent.

7

Vacuum

THERE IS A BELIEF AMONGST immigrant minority communities that the route to success, typically defined as social mobility, can be achieved through a profession. Many Caribbean, African, Southeast Asian, South Asian, and Hispanic parents place huge reverence on professions such as doctors, lawyers, and positions in accounting and finance. It's an interesting phenomenon and the reasons vary amongst communities. For some it's a source of pride, status if you will; for others it's cultural: your children will look after you when they're old so they should be able to earn good money and provide for older as well as younger generations. Upon arriving in foreign countries, many found themselves in difficult circumstances, sacrificing everything for their children. A good return on that investment, therefore, should be a respectable career.

I certainly bought into this idea. If I was going to apply myself to education, then the outcome would be working for a company and wearing a suit. I recall traveling on the train to a martial arts seminar in Manchester. I was about 19, still at university, and I was sitting in in a carriage that was next to the first-class coach. A Black guy strolled past me and entered the first-class carriage. He was probably in his 30s and was dressed in a dark blue suit with a purple tie. This was probably the first time I had seen someone like me dressed like this. I couldn't stop staring at him "That's what I want to be," I said to myself.

The workplace, therefore, represented several things. First, it was an escape, freedom from the financial strain that had colored much of my life. Secondly, I believed that if I managed to work for one of these companies, good things would happen. Part of the belief among minority communities is that professions are full of good people, that with education and higher social status comes a degree of benevolence. The workplace can seem to present an opportunity to escape inequality and to experience a more positive environment. Institutions themselves can also portray themselves as an oasis, corporate brands extolling the virtues and their product or services, as if people entering these institutions can only benefit from working in such a positive environment. The finance industry is particularly focused on this idea, believing it is meritocratic. If you have the ability, you can succeed. If you fail, unfortunately, you are not up to the task. The reality, however, is somewhat different. Institutions do not operate in a vacuum; rather, they reflect and can even amplify wider societal inequalities.

The first issue is one of access and it demonstrates how societal inequality has a correlation with workplace inequality. In 2020, the executive search firm Spencer Stuart produced a report detailing diversity in the S&P 500. Black professionals accounted for only 11% of new directors over the past year and people of color made up just 20% of all board members. Similarly, in the UK in 2021, executive search firm Green Park produced a report that revealed there wasn't a single Black person in the role of board chair, chief executive officer, or chief financial officer in Britain's biggest 100 companies. Navigating the corporate environment requires the ability to access and then progress within organizations. The tendency is to focus on the social obstacles within firms. This might be the interview process, a lack of sponsorship, or promotion criteria. These can be hindrances. But we must also understand the wider context that is the culmination of historic economic inequality. For example, Baby Boomers—the generation born between 1944 and 1964—are expected to transfer $30 trillion in wealth to younger generations over the next 20 years in the US. Having amassed this wealth in the postwar years, it is estimated they control 70% of all disposable income.[1] In the UK, it is estimated the Baby Boomer generation controls around 80% of private wealth.[2] This wealth has been generated through a mixture of stock market returns and house price inflation.

In addition to Baby Boomers themselves, the main beneficiaries of this wealth accumulation are their children. In the UK, property ownership is expected to account for 70% of all transferred wealth.[3] It is this wealth that affords access to better education and healthcare, and also provides knowledge about which career path to follow. Social networks are often forged along economic lines, and this can often lead to routes into institutions through sponsorship, introductions, or familial ties. Black communities, by contrast, have often been excluded from this wealth accumulation. This might be through redlining in the United States or the ability to gain a mortgage in the UK. We categorize these as isolated challenges, but we can see this inhibits the ability to gain both access and knowledge, to seize opportunities, or to build wealth through property ownership.

My first-ever job was in a supermarket. I worked in two stores for a period of five years, from the moment I was able to work at age 16 until I found my first job after graduating university at age 21. Both stores were based in leafy areas of London with housing prices I could only dream of affording. There were two categories of people who worked in the supermarket: the full-time staff who worked on the shop floor and the checkouts, and the part-time workers like me who were usually students. Among the part-time workers there were again two categories. There were those who lived in the area; they didn't really need to work, but their parents felt strongly they should have some "real-life" experience. And then there were us, usually Black and Brown kids who lived in poorer areas but would travel by bus to the affluent areas of Muswell Hill and Crouch End. My experience working in these areas was incredibly insightful. I couldn't help but overhear the conversations of the shoppers in the store. How angry a lady was with her architect. How a daughter couldn't decide between Oxford or Cambridge. Which ski resort a family had just visited. We workers were invisible, ghosts, only to be seen when a customer wanted to know where the peanut butter was, or why we had moved the shampoo.

Although the student workers all dressed in the same uniform and were paid the same hourly rate, our experience of working in the supermarket was very different. The "real-life" students often disappeared during the summer to gain work experience in banks or law firms, or building social impact projects in far-flung places. Often this work was unpaid, but they understood the value. Time off was hard to come by, but they were quite safe in the knowledge that if they couldn't find another part-time job, it wasn't the end of the world. I recall speaking to some of my co-workers and marveling at their attitude. They just had this assurance that everything would work out in their favor. By contrast, for those like me the part-time job was a lifeline, so the thought of taking time away would threaten my ability to even attend university.

One of my closest friends attended the same college as me. We were both studying A Levels, but even affording the bus fare and buying lunch was difficult. He had no family money to fall back on and struggled to find a part-time job. To continue attending university, he resorted to stealing books from the local bookstore and selling them at a discount to other students. When he told me how tight things were, I got him an application form to work in the supermarket. We often reflect on where he would be now were it not for that job, because dropping out of school to earn some money had been a serious consideration.

Putting oneself through higher education is incredibly valuable. It taught me about sacrifice, resilience, and work ethic. But unfortunately, this experience was not valued by others. The financial service recruiting managers I met after graduating and applying to their firms had a different reference point. Their definition of achievement was flying to a "poor country" and doing something they felt was meaningful, like building a school in Africa, or feeding poor children in India. This is also an example of why representation matters: not just because it might inspire others but because if they had had a similar experience to me, they might have seen value in the attributes I had developed.

This economic disadvantage is compounded by social factors. In 2019, researchers from the Centre for Social Investigation (CSI) at Nuffield College, Oxford, found that British citizens from ethnic minority backgrounds send on average 60% more job applications to get a positive response from employers compared to their White counterparts. The researchers sent around 3,200 fake job applications for both manual and nonmanual jobs, from chefs and shop assistants to accountants and software engineers. All the fictitious candidates were British citizens and had moved to UK by the age of six and had identical CVs, cover letters, and years of experience. The only difference was the names of the applicants, which were changed to reflect the candidate's ethnic background. While 24% of British applicants received a call back, only 15% of ethnic minority applicants did. I did receive invitations to interview when I applied to finance firms, but I suspect I was helped by the fact that my name is Anglicized. Only when I arrived for an interview did it become apparent that Gavin Lewis is in fact a Black man.

This inability to access the corporate world also has broader repercussions than just securing a role. It impacts the expectations of minorities. As a Black person, you are constantly told by other Black people, but also learn through personal experience, about how challenging it is to find a role. So your target becomes just getting a foot in the door. Rather than seeking a front-office role, or a position that could have the promise of progression, we are often satisfied with simply being there. While my White friends who graduated university were being incredibly choosy about what role they would or wouldn't do, I was sending out application forms to any firm that was hiring. While my White friends set a minimum for how much their starting salary would be, I didn't even have an idea of what the salary should be. If you have never worked in the environment, if you don't know anyone who has and your reference point are friends who didn't attend university, your expectations are very different.

I graduated university in the summer of 2000, but after four months of seeking a role, I became increasingly desperate. Having experienced poverty growing up, but also seeing my mother struggle to secure employment after completing her degree, I feared not finding a role. The panic began to set in. I had set my sights on finance, but this felt increasingly unlikely, so I reasoned that a role working for the finance sector might be a good step. I had been working closely with a few recruiters, and they questioned whether I would consider a role in recruitment. I resisted at first, but the idea began to grow on me the longer I applied to work in finance without success.

I spent five years working in recruitment, first recruiting IT professionals into banks, then sales professionals into asset managers. My recruitment career taught me a lot, including how to build relationships and how to sell. Some of the people I recruited for and candidates I placed remain good friends and contacts to this day. Such is the power of relationships that one of the firms I recruited for actually hired me as a sales director. But I still held the ambition to work for a financial services firm. When I made the decision to leave recruitment, I first tried to enter the executive search industry and then finance. Reactions were mixed. Close friends were positive. But neither industry could "see" me working for them and questioned whether I would be a "cultural fit."

The *Cambridge English Dictionary* defines culture as "the way of life, especially the general customs and beliefs of a particular group of people at a particular time." In the anthropological sense, the accepted definition was stated by Sir Edward Burnett Tylor, an English anthropologist and founder of cultural anthropology, who described culture as "the complex whole, which includes knowledge, belief, art, morals, law, custom and any other capabilities and habits acquired by man as a member of society."[4] Culture is the glue that binds groups of people together. We may think about this in relation to nation-states, social groups, or minority communities, but companies have also developed culture. An article in the *Harvard Business Review* described corporate culture as the tacit social order of an organization; it defines what is encouraged, discouraged, accepted, or rejected within a group. The late business guru Peter Drucker once said, "Culture eats strategy for breakfast," meaning that firms may have a great strategy, but it is the culture of a firm that determines how successful the strategy and firm will be.

Firms are often incredibly protective and proud of their culture, which has several implications. First, we must assess where company culture is derived. For some firms this will have been developed over time—this could be decades or even centuries. The longer its culture has been in place, the more entrenched it is. Think back to how the first coffee shops were created and the importance of word of mouth in developing relationships in finance. The industry has certainly been professionalized. The importance of introductions gives many a head start, but also determines who gets in and who doesn't. In my experience, that was the "real-life" supermarket workers.

Second, there is the idea of "cultural fit." Even firms that have been created more recently understand the importance of culture. The challenge is that this culture has often been conceived and implemented by a narrow demographic that has rarely included Black people. It's important to note that when an individual joins a firm, the onus is on them to adapt to the company culture. But a firm should assess whether their culture affords maximum productivity from its employees. Presumably they have been hired because of their skills and attributes. If the culture hinders them from fully utilizing those skills and yet the firm needs this individual's abilities, then there is a case for that culture to evolve.

My desire to enter finance was partly driven by the challenge and sense of achievement I felt it would give me. But it was also an escape, a refuge from the poverty that had characterized much of my upbringing. The opportunity to earn money was really an opportunity to improve my life outcomes. If we are to reduce the economic inequality that exists, equal access to opportunities that can change life outcomes is a must.

After six months of searching online every day, meeting people for countless coffees, I finally got a break. A start-up asset-raising firm was willing give me a three-month contract, which eventually became a permanent position. This meant taking a significant pay cut from my recruitment career. Six months of not working had also left me in a lot of debt but it was an opportunity to which I couldn't say no. I worked in the start-up for three and a half years, the 2008 Global Financial Crisis placing strain on a start-up organization. But I had the experience I needed and from there I entered the mainstream asset management industry.

The workplace does not offer a sanctuary from societal inequality. Socially, the experience of the Black professional makes it challenging to progress and partly explains why there is a paucity of Black professionals at the C-suite. But it's the interaction with the economic consequences that are often overlooked. We typically think of property and assets as the main driver of wealth accumulation. I've always wrestled with the fact that if the Baby Boomer generation holds so much wealth, how can Black communities possibly catch up? However, when we assess why the gap persists, we need to understand that wealth is also driven by an accumulation of savings over time. Higher salaries and savings rates could be the key to reducing the gap. This changes the role of the workplace to being an integral part of the solution.

Women have been paid less than their male counterparts in the workplace for decades, with reasons ranging from women being employed in less lucrative industries or roles, disrupted working patterns due to pregnancy and childcare, women being more likely to be in part-time roles, and outright discrimination. In 2017, the UK Government introduced mandatory gender pay gap reporting (GPG) with the aim of reducing, then eliminating, the pay gap between men and women. Results have been mixed. GPG reporting was never going to resolve all the challenges women face in the workplace. Figures from the Office of National Statistics (ONS) show the pay gap was already in decline before the measures were introduced, falling by a quarter between 2011 and 2021. But between 2017 and 2021 the gap narrowed by just 5%, although this can be at least partly attributed to regulation. Firms that do not report currently face no fine or censure. And the impact of the pandemic on women in the workforce has widened the gap again. Nevertheless, the fact that companies have had to report their data has driven the role and progression of women in the workplace to the top of the agenda.

Taking a data-driven approach might therefore afford more targeted diversity and inclusion strategies. The issue of Ethnicity Pay Gap (EPG) reporting has been discussed in the UK but as yet the government has refrained from introducing any legislation. Again, this alone would not resolve the complex challenges that Black employees face, but it should be seen as a part of a wider solution. The workplace is where the majority of individuals earn their income and given the disparity between Black and White households, understanding the pay differential is an imperative.

For this to work, it must be implemented alongside the reduction of social challenges. Some of my experiences of racism in the workplace can only be described as overt racism. In my first role in the supermarket, we would discard used boxes by putting them in large containers in the warehouse, which was hidden behind the shop floor. These were probably about seven or eight feet high, and the cardboard tended to get caught at strange angles. We were often asked to climb up on the containers and squash the cardboard down—a health and safety nightmare. On one occasion I was doing this and the manager of the store walked in, looked up at me, and said, "You were doing that 50 million years ago," presumably in reference to Neanderthal man.

In my first role in recruitment, the security guard at the front desk of the city-based office asked to inspect my security pass every day, even after I had used the electronic scanner to pass through the gate. I thought this was just part of the process until one day a White colleague entered at the same time. While she simply walked past the security guard, he still stopped to see my pass. I looked at him, bemused, and told him that I worked for the same company as my colleague. He replied, "I don't care, I still need to see your pass." I entered the lift with my colleague, who had seen the incident; she looked at me awkwardly and only asked why he was asking to see my pass.

I could fill this book with incidents that have occurred while working in the finance industry. I have been called foreign, likened to the help, and have been called a criminal. What is more pernicious, however, were the experiences that are not obviously related to race. These could be what on the surface are small things, what we call microaggressions. I've attended numerous meetings where the other attendees have stayed rooted to their seats because they weren't expecting a Black person to be in my position. I have attended meetings and conferences where I've been mistaken for the staff serving food or as security. When expressing discomfort when I was younger, disdain as I matured, and offense now, the response is typically the commentator taking offense that I might be offended. These experiences are incredibly damaging—mentally, emotionally, and physically. The stress Black professionals endure when tackling racism releases the same stress hormone—cortisol—that shortens lifespans when facing violence or racism outside of the office. Studies have also found that this only increases the more senior Black professionals become, a phenomenon known as diminishing returns.

We must also understand the economic implications. When you join a corporation, you are handed an employee manual that explains the policies and procedures of the organization. It might contain the dress code, how to take leave, and the complaints process. What you are not told, however, are the unwritten rules: who you should know, who has influence, how to manage your career. In other words, how to fit in and then progress within the company culture. I have also often found that despite my best attempts, there is another set of rules that applies to Black people. .

I have had numerous conversations with Black women about their experiences in the workplace. They are at the epicenter of disadvantage, being both female and Black. Many have said to me, "At least you're a man," to which I reply, "But I'm not." I can't be a whole person. At 6-foot-2, I have to make myself smaller by physically stooping, speaking at a higher octave so my voice isn't too deep, and not shaking a hand too hard. One wrong step and I'm intimidating or threatening or need to learn the company culture. It's impossible to feel that you can be yourself, that you can be safe. It's simply impossible to achieve inclusion, let alone diversity, if your Black employees don't have psychological safety. The disturbing thing about this is that many don't even know they suffer from a lack of it. Not being oneself is just the way it is. This undoubtedly affects performance.

One of most difficult things I listen to is when other Black professionals tell me about their experiences in the workplace. Many say they are not having a negative experience because the company "leaves them alone" or they're "not being treated badly." The benchmark for the Black professional is the absence of bullying, not the presence of sponsorship. This should be the minimum expectation, not the standard we set ourselves. Yet this belief means we don't push for more. As a result, our managers don't select us for stretch assignments or see us as promotion material, confirming a preexisting bias. It then becomes self-fulfilling; many Black professionals I have spoken to have become reluctant to apply for a promotion or put themselves forward for stretch opportunities. All of this impacts the level of income we are able to generate as we don't fulfill our earning potential. Employers do not get the best out of their Black professionals. Companies do not perform to their full potential.

Numerous studies have made the case for businesses increasing the representation among underrepresented groups, including *Harvard Business Review*'s article "Making Differences Matter: A New Paradigm for Managing Diversity" (1996) and McKinsey's series of studies "Why Diversity Matters" (2015), "Delivering through Diversity" (2018), and "Diversity Wins: How Inclusion Matters" (2020). Each have made the case for greater representation, with the McKinsey studies in particular focusing on diversity increasing the likelihood for outperformance. Companies with more than 30% women executives were more likely to outperform by 10 to 30% companies with fewer female executives. And companies with greater ethnic and cultural diversity were more likely to outperform companies with less diversity. In 2019, those companies in the top quartile for ethnic and cultural diversity outperformed the profitability of those in the bottom quartile by 36%. Some companies have benefitted from increased diversity, however, and they had a number of things in common, including ensuring representation of diverse talent, especially in executive management, technical, and board positions; strengthening leadership accountability and capabilities for diversity, equity, and inclusion; enabling equality of opportunity through fairness and transparency; and tackling microaggressions and fostering belonging through unequivocal support for multivariate diversity.

If these initiatives had been in place at earlier points in my career, it might have made my path easier. And I do have hope that younger professionals have an easier route than I did. But I couldn't escape the fact that progress was slow, too slow, and it would take something extraordinary to really move the dial. When I first read these reports, I expected things to change. Finance in particular is driven by performance, so how could the industry forgo such as opportunity? McKinsey themselves stated that despite the seemingly compelling business case, progress hasn't been as expected. In their 2014 data set based in the United States and UK, female representation on executive teams rose from 15% in 2014 to 20% in 2019. Across their global data set, which starts in 2017, gender diversity increased by just one percentage point, from 14 to 15% in 2019. The representation of ethnic minorities on US and UK teams was 13% in 2019, up from just 7% in 2014.

Change, therefore, needs to come from several places: a driven executive team, clients, and regulators. But we may also need to look at different metrics. Pay gap reporting can provide another quantitative measure of the progression of Black professionals alongside qualitative diversity, equity, and inclusion strategies. The take-up of pay-gap reporting to date has been slow. Maybe we need an additional incentive. It also needs to be understood in the context of the life journey of an individual. It is part of the solution along with resolving education, healthcare, and criminal justice inequalities. Crucially, if firms understand the importance of reducing socioeconomic inequality and the impact this has on company performance, progress might be accelerated.

8

Ghosts

WHEN GROWING UP IN A city such as London, it's easy to assume the rest of the world is the same, that everywhere is diverse. It's also easy to assume that poverty is only what you have experienced and that other communities have it easier. One of my concerns about making a case to reduce the racial wealth gap is that people outside of the Black community might not care. I do believe we can evidence the fact that the economic progress of Black communities will benefit wider society. But upon my travels outside of London, two things have occurred to me. The first is that inequality is widespread, experienced across a host of geographies, races, and classes. Second, despite the differences among these communities, there are a lot of parallels between the different groups. As a result, it's not just the economic progress of Black communities that will benefit others, but the possibility of a multiplier effect. If we can find a method that could be employed across a host of disadvantaged communities, the benefit will be increased significantly.

Working for a global corporation often requires traveling to different offices or client locations. London is a cosmopolitan city of 9.5 million people, with over 40% identifying as Asian, Black, or mixed heritage or other.[1] There are enclaves and suburbs where different demographics dominate: Pakistanis in Southall, Jews in Golders Green, or Turks in Green Lanes. New York is similar. London at 607 square miles actually has a bigger footprint than New York's 468 and also has a larger population than New York's 8.2 million.[2] Nevertheless, New York is also truly diverse. It is estimated that up to 800 languages are spoken in New York, the city boasts the largest Jewish population outside of Israel, and 36% of the population were born outside of the United States.[3]

We rarely traveled abroad as a family; an overseas holiday was way beyond our means. University would have been the opportune time to do this but the thought of putting myself in more student debt deterred me from even considering the idea. So much of what I saw outside the limits of London came after I started working in the fund management industry though business travel.

My first experience of business travel was far from glamorous. As a UK salesperson, my destinations were the far flung reaches of England, Scotland, and Wales. This meant I spent much of my time waking up in the early hours of the morning and jumping on the tube to Kings Cross, Paddington, or Euston train stations. One perk was that the journeys were often long enough to warrant a first-class seat. These were often frequented by other people traveling for business, but I would often be the only Black person in the carriage. During one journey to the south of Wales, I was returning from a meeting, and the train employee was serving food and drinks. These were complementary in first class, and you could eat sandwiches or biscuits, or drink teas and coffees. Every time he passed by he asked if I wanted anything, but gave me a lingering look. I didn't think too much about it, until he finally stopped and asked sheepishly, "Are you a footballer?"

During another trip to the south of England, I had arranged to visit my client in a local pub. This often caused some nervousness for me because not only would I stick out like a sore thumb, but I never knew what kind of reaction I would receive. I often envisaged a crowded pub falling silent and heads turning to stare at me when I walked through the door. As I walked to the door of the pub on this trip, an older guy was sitting outside the pub studying a newspaper. He saw me coming and looked up, but then did a double-take and shouted with glee, "It's Barack Obama," before returning to his newspaper. In one sense, I was pre-pared for this, having attended a predominately White school and now working in a predominately White industry. Fending off casual racism had almost become a skill. You either ignore, make light of, or confront the issue, though one has to be choosy about which of these to apply. Too much confrontation means you eventually get worn down by the fight; too much looking past the issue eats away at you as a person and as a human. What I wasn't prepared for, however, was the White people I would find outside of London. Looking back now, I see that I was naïve. I was used to the poverty that surrounded me in London, to the extent that I barely noticed it anymore. But I thought the towns and cities outside of London would be wealthy.

During one trip to Wales, when I reached my destination, the train station was fairly nondescript. I wrapped my scarf around my neck to protect me from the cold. My client's office was another 30 minutes away by car, so I followed the signs to the taxi rank. A group of men sat outside a café next to a long line of blue taxis. When I approached the driver of the first taxi, he greeted me and asked me where I was headed. When I told him he said, "Oh right," then asked when I would be returning. I explained that the meeting was only scheduled for one hour and he said, "Great I'll wait for you outside. Make sure you only use me, please," and he gave me his card. "I'll be right here." He said this three or four times. This was really strange to me. In London I found it impossible to get a taxi, suit or no suit. The trademark black cabs of London would often sail past me, stopping a few hundred yards down the road for another passenger. But here was a taxi driver almost desperate for a fare.

I arrived at my client's offices about 20 minutes early, so thought I would take a walk around the town center. Again, this was a shock to me. The quickest way to the town center was through the car park and past the delivery entrance for a supermarket. As I began to turn a corner, I saw a group of young kids, about 14 or 15 years old, sitting on a railing, heads covered in baseball caps and hoods with cans of what looked like cider strewn around them. One of the kids sat on an old BMX bike; another took a long drag on a cigarette. This was in stark contrast to me, wearing a suit, a long coat, and well-shined shoes. Some of the kids did notice me but paid me little attention. Maybe they were used to businesspeople exiting the nearby offices. I, however, found it hard not to stare. I found myself thinking like a parent. Shouldn't these kids be in school? How are they drinking at 11 o'clock in the morning!?

I carried on walking through to the town center and my surprise continued. Instead of a bustling high street, I was greeted by a parade of shops but with the first two units boarded up and covered in graffiti. The third was called Discount Shop and the next was a café. I debated whether I should grab a coffee from the café but thought it wise to do some reconnaissance. I casually walked past, looked inside, and saw about three tables with groups of men sitting around.

There is nothing strange about this, except I could feel the depression emanating from their faces. They looked long and drawn out, with eyes barely looking at one another. The other residents walking through the town center also had the same look on their faces.

I returned to my client's offices taxi stand, and the taxi took me to the office where I had my meeting. Once the meeting had finished, I exited the office lift and the taxi driver was waiting for me in the lobby; he was determined not to lose his fare. Had I not walked through the town center, I might have questioned why he was so eager for the return fare, but it was clear that this was an economically deprived community. I asked him how business was, and he began to describe how hard it was. The number of taxi drivers had been more than the number of passengers who needed taxis for years, since the steel and coal production industries collapsed in the 1980s and 1990s. Since then, there had been no jobs and this resulted in generations of families being out of work.

Statistics from Save the Children, a UK charity, revealed that Wales has some of the highest rates of poverty in the UK. Figures compiled from 2019–2020 showed that 31% of children living in Wales lived in poverty compared to 30% in England and 24% in Scotland. The Welsh-born economist Gerry Holtham states that Wales has always been the poor relative to England and Scotland. In the pre-industrial era, Wales lacked arable land; coupled with a low population density it proved difficult to achieve rapid growth. There were periods when Wales was able to participate in growth driven by capitalism. In the 1820s and '30s, Wales had two of the largest industrial plants in the world, located in Cyfawith and Dowlais. But these were based on extractive industries and funded by foreign capital. When this capital left, so did the money. The communities left behind had no means to generate income and without ownership of any assets there was no wealth to sustain them, and the class system in the UK made it difficult to progress.

Parts of Wales have therefore also had the experience of rentier capitalism—this economic deprivation leading to higher rates of crime and unemployment, lower educational attainment, and poorer physical and mental health outcomes. This presents the prospect of a solution possibly being applied to different communities and regions. But we need to be mindful of the differences.

There is no universal definition of Britain's class system, but a study conducted in 2011 is often heralded as the best approximation. The Great British Class Survey of 325,0000 White adults revealed that class in the UK is a combination of economic capital such as income and assets, social capital such as social status and friendships, and cultural capital such as cultural interests. The survey also revealed there are seven classes: a wealthy elite, a prosperous middle class, a class of technical experts, new affluent workers, the traditional working class, a precariat who have low levels of capital, and an emergent working class.[4] Associated with the "higher" classes are better life outcomes including health, well-being, and educational attainment. According to the survey, social mobility is achievable and the best way to achieve this is to attend an elite university, one of the UK's Russell Group, and then to find a job in London. I always identified as working class when growing up but due to attending a Russell Group university and working in the city, I am now socially mobile. The biggest catalyst to this social mobility has been economic capital. Social and cultural capital are by-products of living in a more affluent neighborhood and associating with the locals. The social and cultural capital might help you gain more economic advantages, such as being introduced to new business opportunities by a more expansive network, but one cannot live off this.

Social mobility should therefore be broken down to its component parts, and we should first think about economic mobility. I have met many White professionals over the years who grew up in similar places to South Wales. Some discuss their upbringing openly, accents often giving away their heritage. Others, however, tell me in secret and wouldn't dare mention in public that they too were disadvantaged. This is an indictment of corporate culture, that many White professionals feel they cannot be their true selves at work. They gained economic mobility due to being incredibly bright or having a determined parent. The difference for them, however, is their ability to amass social and cultural capital. As White people working in finance, co-workers immediately assume they attended a private school. Many have reached the upper echelons of the industry, only to reveal their backgrounds when it is deemed safe to do so. Yet I have found that social and cultural capital harder to accumulate, and even when I have finally entered different rooms there is one thing I can't escape: being Black. I'm often the only one and get mistaken for, well, a footballer. Pulitzer Prize–winning journalist Isabel Wilkerson likens this to a caste system, and socially Black people will always occupy the lower tier.[5] We may be able to gain economic capital but must understand that we will still have to strive for social and cultural capital.

The Commonwealth of Australia is the largest country in Oceania, a region that comprises thousands of islands that cross both the South and Central Pacific Ocean. Other countries within Oceania include New Zealand, Tonga, Samoa, and Fiji. Over 450 languages are spoken in the region with a truly diverse mixture of ethnicities, including Indian, Papuan, Maori, European, and Indigenous Australian.[6] The Indigenous Australians have inhabited Australia for approximately 65,000 years. Their lives only became intertwined with Europeans in the 17th century, first with the arrival of Dutch explorers and then the British, who claimed the eastern half of the country in 1770.

I remember learning at school about the English explorer Captain James Cook, who set sail in 1768 for the South Seas with secret orders from the British Admiralty to seek "a Continent of Land of great extent" and to take possession of that country in the name of the King of Great Britain. After the "discovery" of Australia, a penal colony was settled in what would become New South Wales beginning on January 26, 1788.[7] Cook's journey to Australia took two years to complete, while today the flight from London to Sydney, Australia, takes approximately 22 hours. My journey to the country, therefore, had little in common with Captain Cook's, apart from the fact that my two-week business trip afforded me a weekend to explore, which just happened to fall on January 26, National Australia Day.

I wasn't quite sure what to expect upon my arrival in Australia. For Britons it seems to be an attractive destination to vacation, work, and even live. I have friends and colleagues who have moved to the country, attracted by the weather and work opportunities but also cultural familiarity. It was for this reason that I perhaps expected a feeling of home away from home. However, the sheer distance from the UK to Australia did make me wonder how familiar it would be to me. I first landed in Melbourne, which has the 10th largest immigrant population among the world's global cities, with residents from over 200 countries and territories.[8] I then traveled to Sydney, which is eighth on the list according to the 2016 census, with 42.9% of the population being born overseas. Both cities certainly felt cosmopolitan, Whites and Asians being the most visible.

But for me it was the first time I visited a major city and felt that I stood out. Some of the other cities with the largest immigrant populations include London, Paris, Toronto,

New York, and Los Angeles. These feel like you could be from anywhere in the world and you could blend in. You might suggest that, because Australia doesn't have a history of migrant Black populations, I shouldn't be surprised. But it does have a history of Indigenous people, yet during my first week I didn't see a single one. This might partly explain why I received so many stares, which in a global city felt extremely odd. Actually, let me be clear: it always feels odd when people stare at you, but if I travel to a smaller town, I almost expect it. This, however, I wasn't prepared for. I thought my free weekend would give me the perfect opportunity to research and try to visit some of the areas where the Indigenous population lived. My internet search revealed a host of things to do for National Australia Day — parades, parties, speeches by celebrities and government officials — until I stumbled across an alternative: National Invasion Day.

I decided to walk around Melbourne and take in both the National Australia Day protest and the alternative. The UK average temperature ranges from 39 to 74 degrees Fahrenheit,[9] while in Sydney it ranges from 47 to 80 degrees Fahrenheit, but it can reach as much 90 degrees Fahrenheit in the summer months.[10] So it was very hot that day. It might have been smarter to find some transport to get around, but walking is the only way to really absorb a city, the sights, the smells, the people. After only a few minutes into my walk from the hotel to the "official" celebration, which was being held in Sydney's Hyde Park, I began to sweat profusely. I had had the foresight to bring a damp washcloth with me, which was a lifesaver until I was able to reach some shade.

Many nations are proud and Australia is no different. The glee on people's faces as they celebrated was palpable. There were flags flying and trumpets being blown; it looked like a real celebration. After I cooled down, I continued my journey. Before I could actually see anything, I could hear the drums and the muffled sound of someone speaking into a megaphone. As I neared the sounds, I was joined by others, and as I rounded a long paved pathway, the scene came into sight. A large group of people were gathered around an older woman who was leading a chant, which was being followed by a captivated audience:

"Always has been, always will be, Aboriginal land. Always has been always will be, Aboriginal land."

People were wearing red, black, and gold T-shirts, the colors of the Australian Aboriginal flag, with various messages written across them. I was struck by the scene and in particular a group of guys who wore T-shirts stating, "White Australia Has a Black History."

I approached the group and asked them if they could give me background on the protest, wondering how, despite standing in the glaring sun, they didn't have a bead of sweat on them. One of the protestors proceeded to tell me what Aboriginals faced daily. He explained that despite Aboriginals being the Indigenous people of Australia, 6 out of 10 White Australians had never met a person of color. He felt the country only wanted to hear from them during the Commonwealth Games and that people crossed the road when he approached. My head was reeling, although not because I was surprised; these were the first Black people I had seen and spoken to despite being in the country for a full week. I was reeling because their experience was so similar to my own. Luke stated that Aboriginals were more likely to be imprisoned, more likely to suffer from mental health issues, and more likely to die in police custody.

The drum beat and chanting stopped and an older women took hold of a microphone. Her greying hair was contrasted against a sculpture of seven bullets, four of which were standing and three lying fallen to the ground. I later learned that this sculpture was by Tony Albert and was unveiled on March 31, 2015. The artwork is called *Yininmadyemi*, which is taken from the Indigenous language of Sydney and translates as "Thou Didst Let Fall." It is an acknowledgment of the Aboriginals and Torres Strait Islanders. The older woman began to discuss what she and her family had been through. Between 1910 and the 1970, many First Nations children, those of Australian Aboriginal and Torres Strait Islander descent, were forcibly removed from their families due to government initiatives to assimilate them in White culture in the belief that their lives would be improved. The Australian government estimates that between one in three and one in ten native children were forcibly taken from their families.[11]

The plight of Indigenous people is often overlooked. Communities in South and North America have also been decimated. Despite the challenges that Black communities in the UK and the US face, we are mobilized and can exert influence at the highest levels of politics, academia, and business. When I heard that the woman was still searching for her children, I could see how raw the wounds still were. Centuries earlier, Black families were broken up during the slave trade and there remains today a legacy of the breakdown of the Black family, which I experienced first-hand. Any solution we create must also fight for those who are yet to be fully recognized.

After a number of speeches, the protest began to walk through the park. As I headed back toward my hotel, the sounds of the drum faded into the background noise, I noticed another group of people standing next to an immense statue of Captain Cook, who is clutching a telescope and staring into the distance. They probably had no idea about the protest and maybe no idea about the experiences of the people whose plight was so apparent. They were almost spirits, ghosts, only to be revealed when someone sought them out.

My wife is French-Vietnamese and our marriage has been a cultural learning experience. My father-in-law was Vietnamese; he left Vietnam for France in 1965. In contrast to my mother, he arrived as a student attending a grand école, a group of leading French educational institutions. Given that Vietnam was a former French colony, there is a large population living in France; there is another large population on the West Coast of the United States. It is estimated that about 400,000 Vietnamese live in France,[12] and 1.4 million live in the United States, making them one of the largest Asian communities in both countries.[13] My father-in-law married my mother-in law, who is White French, and had two children.

The experience my father-in-law had when he arrived in France was very different from my mother's, despite arriving in their respective countries around the same time. He recounted that he was welcomed into the country and although there was some reaction from White French people, he felt the move to the country was positive. So much so that the Vietnamese have often been considered a "model minority," which is partly attributed to their high level of integration into French society but also their high levels of educational attainment and career success.

It may be tempting to view certain minorities in this way. When I first met my wife's family, I marveled at how much they had achieved; they were doctors, politicians, financiers with a close-knit sense of community. But the term "model minority" is riddled with issues. Some of the Vietnamese community's professional attainment is due to the legacy of colonialism whereby wealthy Vietnamese often sent their children to elite schools in France; the first migrants who arrived just after World War I and the second migrants who arrived after the fall of Saigon already had a cultural affinity with France. It is these who are often held up as "models." Other Vietnamese immigrants, however, who were poor or who settled in the United States and Australia, had to work incredibly hard to achieve success against the backdrop of a language barrier and anti-Asian racism. White populations viewed them as a threat to jobs or associated them with the communist Vietnamese threat at the height of the Cold War. Many, therefore, moved into run-down neighborhoods, often alongside Black communities.

When I discuss the success of my wife's family, I can only attribute it to two things: sheer hard work and also a sense of community that remained intact, unlike the Black or Aboriginal familial structure, which was systematically and intentionally taken apart. The comfort my wife's family and community had with one another was palpable, and I was lucky to be part of this. My father-in-law was proud of my achievements, believing in me and providing hope when the clouds gathered. People probably wondered why this little Vietnamese man was walking shoulder to shoulder with this tall Black guy. His passing was difficult, and although we never had a conversation without my wife or mother-in-law translating, I still imagine him there in my corner rooting for me just when I need it most.

When we visited my wife's family in the United States, we traveled to a part of Orange County in southern California that is often referred to as "Little Saigon." There was an abundance of Vietnamese grocery stores, restaurants, and banks owned by and serving the Vietnamese community. It's what I imagined "Black Wall Street" to look like. I could see clearly how the dollar could stay in the Vietnamese Asian community for 28 days. Along with this economic progress, the Vietnamese community experiences better life outcomes.

But this "model minority" also denotes the position many Asians find themselves in. Often Asians are grouped together when in fact they are an incredibly diverse group of encompassing Vietnamese, Chinese, Japanese, and Laotians, to name only a few. The experiences of these groups are also very different from one another. For example, immigrants from Laos experience much higher rates of poverty than other Asian groups. It's also noticeable, however, that despite the success of some, they do not control industries or politics. This has been described as the "bamboo ceiling." They are apparently considered the "model minority" because they are seemingly invisible, not causing any social friction, not causing challenging the establishment. This presents a challenge. Real change for Black communities requires challenging the status quo. And with this comes resistance.

I first visited France during an excursion when I was at school but aside from some vague memories of the Eiffel Tower and the Louvre, I can't really recall much from that trip. My wife is French, and that has allowed me to spend a lot of time in France. When I first arrived at Gare du Nord, one of Paris' six mainline railway stations, to meet my wife's family for the first time, I wasn't quite sure what to expect. So when I disembarked from the Eurostar train and entered the main concourse, I was astounded by the number of Black people I saw. It felt as if there were even more than in London. Now at this point I would reel off some figures about France's ethnic population, but this is actually very difficult. A law enacted in 1872 prohibits distinctions among its citizens regarding their race or their beliefs. This was cemented as recently as 1978 when France proclaimed itself to be "color blind." It seems distinguishing between groups would contravene secular republican principles and would hark back to the days of the Nazi-occupied Vichy era when identity documents were required.

This is, therefore, a very sensitive issue in France, where even discussions about race often remain taboo. But some attempts have been made. In 2004, the French think tank Institut Montaigne estimated that there were 51 million (85%) White people of European origin, 6 million (10%) North African people, 2 million (3.5%) Black people, and 1 million (1.5%) people of Asian origin. In 2015, Michèle Tribalat released a paper estimating the population of ethnic minorities in France in 2011 to be 30% but with ancestry restricted to three generations and an age limit of 60.[14] I was therefore interested to understand the experience of minorities in the country. If the country really is color blind and doesn't differentiate on the basis of race, perhaps this is the answer.

Interestingly, my wife, who is a minority, never had any negative experiences due to her race. For her, being both White French and Vietnamese was positive. She never felt people treated her differently and her Vietnamese heritage only enriched her upbringing. This was important for me as it helped me to realize that people do have different perspectives on things and that being a minority is not necessarily a disadvantage. For her, the challenges I have faced have been difficult initially to understand. Yet she has provided comfort as well as an alternative view when needed.

I was curious, however, to understand the experience of the Black and Arabic communities in France. On one trip, my wife and I were visiting friends and I struck up a conversation with another Black guy. Fortunately, his English was better than my French, so we were able to discuss our relative experiences. What emerged was a familiar story of both explicit and subtle racism and a window into the plight of France's minority communities. But the problem for him was that there was no definition for what he experienced.

In 2016, Adama Traore, a 24-year-old Black man, died in police custody in Beaumont-sur-Oise in northern France, with allegations that he was asphyxiated. In 2017, a young Black man, Theodore Luhaka, age 22, was arrested by police officers in the Paris suburb of Aulnay-sous-Bois. A video of the arrest shows Theo being wrestled to the ground and handcuffed. The officers then abused Theo by forcing a truncheon into his anus, leaving him with severe injuries. Marseille, which is home to a large socioeconomically deprived Black and Arabic community, saw 28 gang-related deaths in 2019 and 23 in 2018.[15] These incidents occurred amid the familiar challenges of lower prospects, higher rates of unemployment, and health issues. All of these incidents have resulted in protest and cries for justice. For a solution to be applied in different countries, it needs to be able to navigate local laws and regulations. Even in the UK and the United States, one of the biggest obstacles is gathering and accessing data. This might sound procedural but without identifying and assessing data, without understanding the situation in these communities, it's incredibly challenging to find a solution, let alone implement one. The Black person I was speaking with said poignantly, "If we don't see race, then we can't name it, then it doesn't exist. We don't exist."

One of the pleasing aspects of my career in finance and the stance I have taken on inequality is meeting the many other talented Black professionals. Being one of a very few Black professionals in most of the organizations I have worked for initially led me to believe that there wasn't anyone else. Companies lament their inability to hire due to "pipeline issues" or an inability to find the right executive. In the UK, there are awards and lists for Black talent at all levels and across a range of industries. The names change every year, which points to a depth that needs to be utilized. In the United States, however, I was taken aback by the scale of the talent. On a business trip to New York, I was invited to a celebration of the iconic Studio Museum Harlem, which collects, researches, and supports artists of African descent. The celebration was a black-tie event and attracted New York's Black artistic, cultural, business, and political elite.

I arrived early, which gave me the opportunity to strike up a number of conversations. What surprised me was the sheer number of Black people in positions of influence. I met CEOs, political aides, investors, and surgeons. I struck up a conversation with an older Black guy, Leon, who sported a striking white beard. He was surprised at my accent and his eyes lit up when he asked, "Oh, you're from London?"

He recounted his numerous visits to the city and said he loved Hyde Park and High Street Kensington, which immediately made me think, "This guy is doing alright." I said I was astounded at the number of professionals in the room, and he explained that it wasn't a fair representation, and that the numbers and the level of influence is much greater in Washington, DC, or Atlanta. This was an important message for me because we tend to think of the Black experience as one of struggle. Perhaps we also need to think about what we have achieved and the power we do actually have.

I asked Leon whether he feels we are making progress, and he said he feels we've come a long way since the 1960s, but he would like to see more ownership of large-scale businesses and assets. Although there is a Black middle class, many Black communities are being left behind and the growth of the Black professional class in the United States has stalled. The statistics seem to bear this out. According to the 2010 US Census, Black households had a median income of $32,068, which placed them within income's second quintile. Of Black households, 27.3% earned an income between $25,000 and $50,000, while 15.2% earned between $50,000 and $75,000, 7.6% earned between $75,000 and $100,000, and 9.4% earned more than $100,000. The problem for Leon is that this felt precarious. He said he knew many families who were doing well but had lost their homes during the 2008 Global Financial Crisis. He felt the Black middle class struggled as they worked incredibly hard to maximise their earnings, but did not have the wealth accumulated over generations, usually through home ownership, to act as a buffer. Plus, they had to deal with all the usual middle-class challenges such as expensive college fees and mortgage payments, all while navigating being Black in America. In the UK, a similar issue occurs with middle-class families called "JAMs," or Just About Managing, often seen as the forgotten class, which is only amplified if you are Black. This was concerning to me. I naively thought that if we bring more Black people into the middle classes, this would perhaps be the biggest opportunity for change. But these communities, who felt relatively successful, were still not immune to centuries of structural economic disadvantage. This reinforced the fact that the structures themselves must evolve. But also, economic progress has to be continuous and not a fixed point.

I left Tottenham at age 15. My mother moved us out of the council estate to another council property in an area called Hornsey. I still had close friends in Tottenham and would visit frequently. But as the years rolled by, we slowly lost contact and I didn't visit the area for many years. I'm now a trustee of a charity that is passionate about regenerating the area so I now go back to Tottenham regularly. But, until recently, I still hadn't been back to the council estate where I grew up. After a day at school, I used to get off the bus and walk the rest of the journey home. As I approached the estate I would be on red alert, ready in case anything happened. It could be someone challenging me, or an aggressive dog that didn't like the way I smelled. My first time back as a grown man, I could feel the tension as I got out of my car. My first impression was how small everything seemed. The estate had always felt imposing, but I was amazed at how nonthreatening everything was. The building was the same, save for some new doors and windows on the individual flats. There is now an entry system that prevents nonresidents from entering. This would have been a lifesaver when I was younger. Most of the fights I had were with kids from outside of the estate.

The demographics of Tottenham have also changed. The row of shops that were synonymous with my childhood now catered to the Kurdish community, and the people I saw coming and going were Eastern European and Asian with the occasional Black person. Seven Sisters tube station in Tottenham has two exits. When I was young, exit two would take you directly onto Tottenham High Road. The sight that had always greeted me was a record shop called Body Music (or as it was rebranded, Every Bodies Music), which was actually more than a record shop. Situated right on the corner, it dominated the high street, almost a gateway into Tottenham from neighboring Hackney. It stocked vinyl, mostly reggae, but more recently hip-hop and R&B, and was a signal of the area's cultural heritage. If you walk up the stairs from exit two today, that shop is no longer there. Perhaps this is result of the onset of digital streaming and the decline of the high street. In its place is coffee shop chain Costa Coffee, and the customers and staff of this location are now predominately Eastern European. West Green Road used to have about three different barber and hair care product shops, which catered to the large Black community. These are gone. Many of the Black residents have moved out.

As I headed back to my car, I was baffled by how stark the change was from when I grew up there. I saw a guy probably in his mid-30s who was walking and I called out to get his attention. He gave me a cautious look, which I expected, but relaxed when I told him I was writing about the area. His name was Kevin and he was born in Tottenham; he was the office manager of a local estate agent. I asked him how the community had evolved, and he described the slow process of change. The influx of Caribbean families had slowed, and many of the more recent arrivals were West African. Many of the Caribbean families had moved out to other inner-city areas such as Enfield where housing was cheaper. But many had moved out of London completely to areas such as Essex and Kent. Eastern European families then moved in and utilized the accommodations.

"OK," I said, "so the area is still poor, it's just a different group of people?" He said yes, except that some areas were being regenerated, but not to benefit of the local community. The houses his company sells are usually to White professionals looking for investment opportunities. Or they move into the area but into gated developments that are self-contained communities with their own shops and transport links. Most of his friends had moved out, and those who were left felt almost alienated. The community had changed, the places where they used to socialize were gone; they had to travel much further to find Caribbean food. Kevin told me that his son had nowhere to go after school because all the playschemes had been shut down.

I got into my car and thought I would have a look for myself. I drove to nearby Tottenham Hale, which had been dominated by a large retail park and industrial sites when I lived there. As I rounded a corner, gleaming multicolored buildings came into view with cranes leering into the sky. Tottenham Hale now has independent shops selling coffee and artisan breads were visible. One part of me could see the investment opportunity. Gentrification has the ability to unlock value in areas that otherwise remain deprived. But if this doesn't benefit the local community, inequity is only increased and poor residents simply move to another cheaper area and experience even greater levels of deprivation. One of the key attributes of economic progress is access. This might be access through a mechanism such as insurance, but it also needs to encompass the built environment. This might entail investing in the local community through quality affordable housing alongside quality schools and healthcare. Regenerating an area where the local community is forced out simply moves an issue elsewhere. I thought back to what Kevin said: "The residents are in Tottenham, but they're not *in* Tottenham. These properties are for them, not us."

9

Plastic Bag

I STILL HAVEN'T WATCHED THE full eight-minute video of George Floyd being murdered. I think I watched about four minutes before I had to turn it off. My initial reaction the first time the clip was sent to me was one of ambivalence, not because of what it entailed but because I have seen this movie before. This isn't the first time that footage of Black people dying at the hands of the police has emerged. On July 17, 2014, Eric Garner was killed in New York after police approached him on suspicion of selling single cigarettes. Eyewitnesses told a different story, that Eric had broken up a fight. But when two police officers arrived, the two men who were fighting had already left. Police surrounded Eric, who protested his innocence and asked the officers why they were continuously harassing him. Sirens can be heard in the background as more officers arrive. One of the officers then grabs Eric by the neck and pulls him to the ground, while the other officers, who now number about eight, cuff him and keep him in a choke hold.

Another officer kneels on the back of Eric's head and pushes it into the ground. The footage ends with Eric lying lifeless on the floor. To write this section I had to rewatch the video and still can't get through the first couple of seconds without crying. Crying because a man who is pleading "I can't breathe" is being suffocated to death. Crying because he is Black and looks just like me. Crying because it reminds me of the time the police officer had me up against the shutters of the corner shop by my neck and I thought was going to pass out.

Cherry, Mark, Theo, Breonna, Christopher, Kingsley, Darren, Sean, Botham, Stephon, Aura, Philando, Alton, Freddie, Adama . . .

These are just some of the names I've heard, read, or been told about who have either died while in police custody or at the hands of the police. In the UK, Black people account for 8% of deaths in police custody even though we only make up 3% of the population.[1] In the United States, Black Americans are 3.23 times more likely than White Americans to be killed by the police.[2] So when the video of George Floyd was sent to me, I couldn't watch it. It was only after I received it from several people that I watched the first four minutes before turning it off.

I wasn't surprised when the news started to emerge that Black people were more susceptible to the coronavirus disease, COVID-19. The pandemic only served to highlight an inequality that had persisted for centuries. Black people in the United States and UK experience worse health outcomes across nearly every metric even though most of the diseases they suffer from are treatable. This novel coronavirus, the first case of which was identified in Wuhan, China, reached the UK in late January 2020. News was swirling but no one had really grasped the magnitude of the situation, so life basically carried on as usual. I attended a conference and spoke at a panel about diversity and inclusion with hundreds of other finance professionals. Aside from bumping fists and using hand sanitizer, the event proceeded pretty much as normal. There was little in way of ventilation in the conference space, no one wore masks, and symptoms were assumed to be a cold, not the actual virus. It was surreal. Only on the last day of the conference did attendees begin to receive messages from their companies to leave the conference and begin working from home. The first lockdown had begun.

The speed at which the corporate world shifted to home working is truly impressive. Within weeks we had adjusted to video conferences, virtual meetings, and closing deals without any human contact. For many this was a difficult period. The barrier between home and work became increasingly blurred. Children had to be schooled at home, missing out on vital social interactions. Women bore the brunt of this and were set back decades in their fight for equality. My attitude was somewhat different. It was hard but not as hard as for some. Whenever I dialed into a call and turned on my camera, most of the faces who looked back at me were White. But when I ventured out to the supermarket, whenever I watched the buses go by, whenever I was able to get back on the tube, the faces who looked back at me were Black and Brown.

In 2020, figures from the UK's Office for National Statistics (ONS) revealed that Black people were four times more likely to die from COVID-19 than White people. The ONS figures found the difference was not caused by genetic differences but a mixture of preventable conditions such as living arrangements and poor health caused by lower educational attainment and wealth inequalities.

Many Black people were unable to seek refuge at home and still earn a living. To survive meant risking their own and their family's health. But even when adjusting for these factors, Black people were still twice as likely to die from COVID-19. And of Black people, men were more likely to die, and of Black men, those with Caribbean heritage were more likely to die. So when one my closest friends sent me a message with news that his father was in hospital with COVID-19, I was upset but not surprised. When he told me his father had passed away, I was devastated for him but not surprised. When the restrictions eased, and higher death rates for Black people persisted for months but no one could tell me why I was more likely to die, I was worried but not surprised.

Israel, a friend with whom I had attended school, had always been in the restaurant trade. He had run fast-food fried chicken and pizza shops. He had opened a new restaurant just before the pandemic, his latest venture, and he used a significant portion of his savings plus a loan from the bank to finance it. The restaurant opened in January 2020 and as in the corporate world, the prospect that we would all be asked not to leave our homes was never entertained. So while I was able to work from home and continue engaging with my clients, Israel plowed more and more of his savings into his business, assuming like many of us this would be short lived and his customers would return. They never did, and he had to move back in with his partner's mum, unable to afford the rent on their flat.

Others fared much worse. Black people in the UK and United States suffered job losses at a much greater rate. The US Census Bureau's Household Pulse Survey found Black unemployment rates were much higher between 2020 and 2021. Much of this stemmed from the higher rate of unemployment Black people suffered even before the pandemic began. But the survey revealed Black adults in households where someone had lost income since the start of the pandemic were more likely to report uncertainty about their ability to pay for their housing than White adults. The survey also found Black adults were more likely to have taken on unsecured debt such as credit cards, loans, or simply borrowing money to pay for household expenses such as rent, energy, and food. Black adults living in households where someone lost employment income were 11.1% more likely to report they did not have enough to eat. And the data also suggests Black adults were more likely to suffer from mental health issues such as anxiety stemming from the health and economic uncertainties.

In 2018, I wrote a blog entitled "Now that I have your attention . . ." documenting my experience growing up in Tottenham and working in the finance industry. It was in part designed to highlight the challenges Black people faced, but also a cry to be heard and seen. In the UK, anyone who wasn't White was captured under the acronym BAME: Black, Asian, and Minority Ethnic. The term lumped together non-homogenous groups, even though the challenges Black people faced were vastly different from the challenges Asians faced. But it also failed to recognize that Black people are not monolithic. There are plenty of Black people reading this book who will identify little with my experience. In same vein, there will be Caribbeans who will have a completely different perspective from West Africans. The same can be said for Indians, Pakistanis, and Bangladeshis captured under the "A."

This was also the height of the #MeToo movement and firms were finally being woken up to the fact that representation and sexism were a problem in the boardroom.

Some progress was being made on this front, and it heralded the rise of diversity and inclusion, but I knew something was amiss when I was contacted by headhunter who sat in front of me and said, "We really like your profile but really want someone diverse." In other words, a White woman. It began to grate when I was told in meetings how diverse the business I worked in was, despite me being the only Black person, and when the industry began to pat itself on the back during award ceremonies for "diversity" and not a single Black or Brown face could be seen. I lamented to my wife about this. She said quite starkly, "Well, you're one of the most senior Black people in the industry. If you don't take a stand, no one else will." The Black representation in my industry is so sparse I could identify most of the other Black people in it. We were brought together out of necessity and decided to announce that Black people do exist and here is our experience.

Dawid Konotey-Ahulu is one of the only senior Black professionals in the asset management industry. He co-founded a successful investment consultancy. We met during the usual course of business, but such was our conditioning that we never discussed the fact that we were Black in a White industry. Darren Johnson, the global chief operating officer for a sustainable equity asset manager, is one of the few Black members of the C-suite in the UK asset management industry. We became business acquaintances, then friends, and traveled to the United States together. But such was our conditioning that we never discussed the fact that we are Black in a White industry. Justin Onuekwusi is a fund manager at a global asset manager and one of only 15 Black fund managers in the UK. We raised money for charity and became friends. But such was our conditioning that we never discussed the fact we were Black in a White industry. Rachel Green is a one of the few Black sales directors in the UK asset management industry. We worked together and became friends. But we never discussed the fact that we were Black in a White industry.

This all changed when Dawid published a blog, "So can we talk? . . . Talkaboutblack' " The title became our tagline, taking apart BAME and claiming our identity. It also discussed the challenges many segments of the Black community face. It identified four hurdles many Black people need to overcome to forge a career in finance: the socioeconomic inequalities that many are born into, the inability to gain entry into the industry, difficulties in progressing once in the industry, and a reluctance in society to confront the taboo subject that is race. All of this manifests in a lack of Black representation in the C-suite. We used the analogy of a hosepipe to describe this, that each hurdle is a kink in the hosepipe. This means there is significant potential in the Black community, but to realize this potential, or let the water flow, you need to unkink the hosepipe. Furthermore, unkinking one part of the hosepipe is not enough and the water, or potential, will get stuck at another point. You need to unkink the entire hosepipe for the water to flow.

Both my blog and Dawid's went viral. It set off a movement that began to address some of the systematic and structural challenges we face as Black professionals. We held talks in front of hundreds of people. We launched mentoring initiatives and school programs, equipping students with the ability to navigate the treacherous graduate recruitment process. We held countless one-on-one meetings with peers and younger Black professionals. We tried to make a difference. I'm sure—well, at least I hope—that we helped some. Our statistics show we have managed to reach thousands, but years of trying to change the environment for others, while no one sought to change ours, began to take its toll. Pressing publish on a blog, speaking at an event, launching a program, writing this book, all feel like significant risks to my career. For every positive reaction, there is someone who disagrees violently with something I've said. Someone who feels I've ignored them because I didn't respond to their message among the dozens I struggle to reply to every week. Someone who gets upset because I used this word instead of that word. One of our early initiatives was to normalize discussions about race. We recorded a panel discussion and Dawid posed the question, "So is the industry racist?" I didn't feel the industry was ready for this discussion. I could see the headlines: "Black Professional Calls Finance Industry Racist." I feared it would make me a pariah. So I replied, "No, it's people's unconscious bias." This is despite an acceptance that sexism was and still is a problem in a finance.

Some have said to me that it comes with the territory; others feel that I've "made it" and that's why I am able to speak out. But #Talkaboutblack isn't my career. The countless meetings where people unload their emotions into me often triggered situations, interactions that I am still processing. It reached a point where people took so much, I had almost nothing left. But if I stopped, I couldn't look my daughters in the eye and tell them I did everything in my power to give them a better chance than I had.

When the video of George Floyd was sent to me, I didn't watch it. Not only had I seen this movie before, but my eyes were raw from watching the sequels and prequels on loop.

The first sign that this time might be different was when social media picked up the video and then the mainstream news did so as well. I spoke to my mum about the George Floyd video and asked her if she felt it was different. She couldn't hide her cynicism, and I had to agree with her. Until another video surfaced. This wasn't a violent death at the hands of the police but an altercation between a Black man, Christian Cooper, and an unrelated White woman, Amy Cooper. Christian was birdwatching in an area of New York's Central Park called the Ramble. In this area, dogs are required to be kept on a leash. Amy was walking her dog but had let it roam free. Christian requested Amy put her dog back in a leash, which Amy refused to do. Christian then tried to coax the dog toward him with a dog treat, to which Amy reacted angrily, "Don't touch my dog!" Christian then started to record the interaction on his phone, at which point Amy dialed 9-1-1 and stated, "There is an African-American man, I'm in Central Park, he is recording me and threatening me and my dog. Please send the cops immediately!" The incident happened the same day as the killing of George Floyd, showing starkly the two sides of racism. I then found out that Amy held a senior role at Franklin Templeton, a global asset manager. This was difficult for me to handle because any attempt to call out racism was usually met with ridicule or denial that anyone in the finance industry could really be racist. But here it was, on film. Within the Black business community, the discussion then went from George Floyd to how many "Amys" we have worked for or with. Both stories began to dominate the news.

I began to receive even more messages, not just about the incidents but about what we, #Talkaboutblack, were going to say or do about them. Social and mainstream media were full of articles, stories, and blogs expressing distress at the events. We were hurting but were reluctant to add to the pain. Weeks went by, and the pressure to respond only increased. I had had time but really didn't have an answer. Rather, I had more questions: Why does this keep happening? Why is my life held in less regard than others? So one evening I sat at the kitchen table, feeling lost, and began to write.

After the events of the last few weeks I'm
without words.
I've found myself questioning who and
what I am.
What am I?
I am more likely to grow up
without a father
I am more likely to be poor
I am more likely to be expelled from school
I am more likely to be victim of
violent crime
I am more likely to be stopped
and searched
I am more likely to be unemployed
I am more likely to be paid less
I am more likely to be racially abused
I am more likely to be judged prematurely
I am more likely to be depressed
I am more likely to be anxious
I am more likely to be sectioned
I am more likely to be told to lower my
expectations
I am more likely to be told I should be grateful
I am more likely to be seen as a threat
I am more likely to be told I am aggressive
I am more likely to die from COVID-19
And yet I am human
I am a son
I am a father
I am a mentor
What are you?

In the original version I wrote *And yet I am a leader,* but after sending this to both Justin and Darren we agreed to humanize the content. Justin suggested we ask people to hold up a sign to a camera and tag five other people asking them to state what they are and for each of those people to tag five more people. I have to be honest; I really didn't believe people would actually go to the trouble of taking a picture, let alone tagging someone else. But I felt that even if they simply read the post, they might understand what we as Black people have to go through. So on a Tuesday morning, Darren, Justin, Rachel, Dawid, and the other founding members of #Talkaboutblack created posts on social media with accompanying pictures.

Within minutes posts started to appear; within hours the power of social media took effect as people began to post their *I AMs*. Some posted as a sign of solidarity with the Black community.

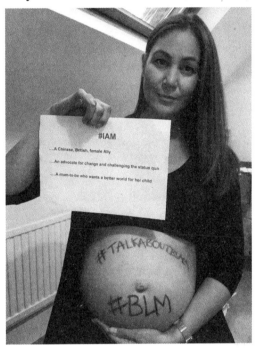

For others it was sign of what they were going through.

The industry press picked up the story and, in our profession, it become a defining movement.

I have mixed feelings about the #IAM campaign. I'm certain it united people and provided an alternative opportunity to a debate that had become incredibly polarized. #BlackLivesMatter was founded in 2013, a response to the acquittal of George Zimmerman, who fatally shot Black teenager Trayvon Martin in Florida in 2012. Zimmerman was charged with second-degree murder after confronting Martin, whom he suspected of criminal activity after a spate of break-ins in his neighborhood. An altercation occurred and Martin was fatally shot. The jury deliberated for 16 hours and rendered a not-guilty verdict.[3]

Black Lives Matter campaigns for the rights of the Black community against a backdrop of police brutality and racism. It is a decentralized organization that gained further prominence following the deaths of Michael Brown in Ferguson, Missouri; Eric Garner in New York City; and George Floyd. Many took issue with the approach and ethos of #BlackLivesMatter, or BLM as it soon became known, with many White people using the rebuttal All Lives Matter. This is intended to minimize the importance of Black lives versus that of others. In response, supporters of Black Lives Matter argued that stating All Lives Matter denies the experience and evidence that Black lives are at greater risk than White. When discussing the issue with friends and colleagues, it felt that there was no middle ground. The issue became one of who was right and who was wrong rather than the problem itself. Perhaps President Barack Obama summed up the debate best in 2015 by stating, "I think that the reason that the organizers used the phrase Black Lives Matter was not because they were suggesting that no one else's lives matter . . . rather what they were suggesting was there is a specific problem that is happening in the African-American community that's not happening in other communities."[4]

A further polarizing issue was "White privilege," the concept that White people are afforded societal advantages over non-White people even if they exist within the same legal and political construct. Like #BlackLivesMatter, the idea of White privilege existed before the death of George Floyd and is rooted in European imperialism and colonialism. For example, academics such as Charles V. Hamilton have researched the relationship between the White supremacy in the transatlantic slave trade and Black subjugation and how they manifest themselves in modern society. Critics of this idea claim that many White people are also disadvantaged, in some circumstances more so than Black people. Again, I can understand the premise. I am privileged; I was fortunate to be born in a country with a free healthcare and education system, and I work in finance and can afford a good standard of living. Yet I can't escape the fact that my color has, and continues to, disadvantage me to a great extent.

The #IAM campaign, therefore, caused me to ponder two questions. We had united people but why had these ideas, which were predominantly debated by activists and academics, divided so many at this particular point in time? It's partly due to circumstance. In 2017 a fire broke out in the 24-story Grenfell Tower block in Kensington in London. The fire was caused by an electrical fault, but cheap and highly flammable materials were used when constructing the building, as they are in many council blocks in the UK. The majority of the 74 people who died were poor and of color. It was news, and a community was devastated. But to most it was just news.

In 2018, it emerged that people were being wrongly detained, denied legal rights, and threatened with deportation. At least 83 people had been deported by the UK's Home Office. Many had arrived from the Caribbean decades earlier as part of the Windrush generation. Hundreds faced deportation despite being British citizens, and many lost jobs, housing, and medical care, and were refused reentry to Britain. These individuals had lived, worked, and paid taxes in England. It sent shockwaves through a community who had regarded the UK as home. But to many it was just news.

But at the time George Floyd was killed, much of the world had paused. Because it was during the pandemic, during lockdowns, many people had the space to actually notice. Yet it was also due to how polarized society had become. Since the Global Financial Crisis of 2008, inequality among poor Black people but also poor White people had increased considerably. Capitalism, which has brought prosperity to so many, had also marginalized many more. The tenets of this, such as globalization and free movement of labor, were effectively rejected by a swathe of the populations in the United States, UK, and Europe through the election of populist governments. If George Floyd represented the inequality faced by Black people, the visceral reaction to the demands of the Black community by poor White people represented the increased marginalization by their White counterparts. The problem is that both groups have been fighting each other while the real culprit—economic inequality—continues to hide in plain sight.

The second question I had was about how many people had actually read my original post. When I speak to people about the campaign, many said they spent hours, sometimes days, trying to figure out what they were. But rarely did anyone comment on the *I am more likely* part of my post. For me, it was this that was important, it was this that was intended to change minds, it was this that was a cry for help, for me, for other Black people. Part of the reaction should have also been why I am more likely to be paid less, be depressed, or be unemployed. And, then while undertaking some research for this book, I stumbled across a photo from almost 55 years ago.

On February 12, 1968, 1,300 Black sanitation workers went on strike in Memphis, Tennessee, due to the dangerous working conditions and low pay they faced while performing their jobs. Unionization among Black workers was forbidden, but after the deaths of two workers, Robert Walker and Echol Cole, who were crushed by a garbage truck, the workers went on strike. One of the civil rights leaders who joined the strike was Martin Luther King Jr. The day before his assassination, he marched with the workers, many of whom wore signs that read: *I Am a Man*. Interestingly, there is another symbolic image that used similar wording. British ceramics maker and abolitionist Josiah Wedgwood around 1787 created an image of a kneeling African who was enslaved that became the signature for the abolitionist movement. Engraved toward the top of the image are the words *Am I not a man and a brother?*

Looking at the two images stirs different emotions in me. The 1968 picture is one of defiance and originated from the Black workers. The abolitionist movement played an integral role in the end of slavery, but I couldn't put my finger on why this image didn't quite feel right. It might be because it depicts a Black man who is enslaved begging for his freedom, but perhaps that was the dominant image of Black people among the British at the time. Then it struck me. It was eerily similar to the sculpture above the Royal Exchange. It tells me we have to take control of our future; no one is going to hand it to us. And that the goal has to be economic freedom alongside social freedom. Until we achieve this, we won't truly be free.

I wasn't the only person who was asking questions following the death of George Floyd. For the first time, large proportions of mainstream society recognized there was a problem. It's easy to hold up a sign on social media, to upload a Black Square in place of your profile pic, and quote #Icantbreathe. The cynic in me wondered if my mother was right and this was my generation's Emmett Till or Rodney King, whether 2020 would be the year of Black people, only to be forgotten when the next crisis occurs. But perhaps one thing was different. I was asked to speak at countless panel sessions and roundtables. I was asked to deliver keynote addresses and conduct too many media interviews. And time and time again I was asked the same question by White attendees: *What can I do?*

At the beginning I tried to provide answers despite taking umbrage at the fact I was being asked to find solutions to a problem that not only did I not create but to which I was still a victim. During one keynote address, the floor was opened to the audience for questions. An older gentleman referred to the blog I had written two years earlier and said, "I'll be honest, I thought you had my attention then, but you really do now." This was a rare moment but for it to count, this societal concern not only has to hit the public consciousness, but it also has to permeate people's everyday existence. Such is the size of the task. I then began to search for similar causes that have moved from the fringes to the mainstream: the anti-smoking campaign, anti-war protests, and then, ah, climate change.

At one point the issue of climate change was considered niche, and those who advocated for controlling rising temperatures were stereotyped as eco-warriors, boarding ships in the Arctic or chaining themselves to trees, with corporations taking little responsibility for the change in climate. Shareholder returns were the order of the day. It has taken a few passionate individuals, some high-profile ambassadors, and a series of natural disasters to move the issue from a belief or values discussion to legislative and business imperative. Businesses now measure climate risk and understand its impact on society. But the real catalyst for this was societal pressure. Climate change is now a risk for which everyone is required to take personal responsibility.

But whereas climate change threatens the existence of those in the boardroom and their children, there remains a belief that inequality does not. Those most impacted by inequality are not at the upper reaches of corporations. Governments need to implement policies. The risk of inequality needs to be measured.

A few high-profile advocates wouldn't hurt, but more than anything it requires society to take responsibility, and this starts with the individual. Many people now recycle, eat less meat, and have stopped using plastic bags. Black communities need to mobilize around the issue of economic inequality. But there will be resistance. And we can't do it alone. So, when it comes to inequality and the issue of race, what are you doing? What is your plastic bag?

10

The Opportunity Index

REDUCING INEQUALITY IS ONE OF humanity's greatest challenges. It has been at the center of protests, revolutions, and wars. More recently it has seen the rise of populism and social movements that have begun reshaping our social, political, and economic landscape. Developed nations have just experienced a 30-year period of economic growth and stable inflation, often referred to as the Great Moderation. This has been against a backdrop of global trade and open borders. We are now wrestling with rising temperatures, a global pandemic, war, economic instability, and rising living costs. Inequality is intertwined with all of these challenges, and the need to reduce it has never been more urgent. Racial inequality is a combination of both social and economic disadvantage. A large proportion of Black communities have never participated in the Great Moderation. The disadvantages they have experienced have persisted despite the gains made by other demographics.

To resolve this, six crucial aspects are required:

1. We must quantify the problem. Without this it's difficult to grasp the size of the issue, or even recognize it. Economic inequality is a result of income, credit, education, funding, and access inequality, often referred to as the racial wealth gap. It is the reduction of these, together, that will provide better health, employment, and opportunity outcomes.
2. Governments and public bodies need to put policies in place that establish the foundation for progress. This means providing Black people wrestling with poverty the means to have their basic human needs met.
3. We need to shift mindsets to focus on the intersection between social and economic inequality and create equity. This means not only tackling the racism seen in someone's attitude or behavior but the racism that prevents Black communities from progressing economically.
4. The private sector needs to work in partnership with governments and public institutions to mitigate risk but also to seize the opportunity.
5. Society needs to own the problem and individuals need to take steps to mitigate inequality risk. This cannot reside solely in the hands of Black activists, community workers, professionals, and allies. The apathetic middle too must take action.
6. A framework must be developed to implement, measure, and demonstrate change.

The primary reason for the racial wealth gap is attributed to the economic loss Black communities suffer due to the legacy of slavery. Most agree about this. But discussions about how to bridge this gap have led to an impasse.

Reparations are often seen as the primary solution. Proponents also feel this will right a long-standing wrong. Many understand the case for reparations, but there is often disagreement about how to fund a program and who pays. There are also many who disagree with the idea of reparations itself through a reluctance to ask today's generations to take responsibility for the past. Perhaps a way forward, then, is to bridge the gap through *investing* in marginalized communities. This might resolve the root economic causes of inequality and provide a benefit for wider society. Furthermore, if we can establish a framework to reduce inequality in Black communities, it raises the possibility of achieving the same for other marginalized groups.

To understand the case for investment requires an understanding of the historical and contemporary discussions about reparations. In 1783, Belinda Royall, a freedwoman, petitioned the commonwealth of Massachusetts for reparations. Belinda had been born in today's Ghana but was sold into slavery as a child and purchased by the Royall family when she reached the American colonies. Her master, Isaac Royall, abandoned her after fleeing to Nova Scotia at the outbreak of the American Revolution. Belinda was in servitude for 50 years but after being freed made her case for compensation. She petitioned to be compensated for the decades serving the needs of her master in comparison to her happy childhood in Ghana. Her argument persuaded the Massachusetts General Court to award her a pension of 15 pounds, 12 shillings per annum out of the estate of Isaac Royall.[1]

This was a revolutionary concept, that the formerly enslaved might be owed something. Abolitionists such as the Quakers endorsed the idea so much so that in New York, New England, and Baltimore, they made membership contingent upon compensating one's former enslaved. As a result, there were additional cases of compensation. In 1782, the Quaker Robert Pleasants emancipated his 78 enslaved and granted them 350 acres. Pleasants later developed a proposal to build a school for the formerly enslaved. In his will, he left an endowment of land and money to establish such a school "for the benefit of the Children and descendants of who have been Emancipated by me, or other black Children whom they may think proper to admit." Despite these precedents, there has never been any wholesale compensation for Black people. In fact, the compensation argument typically heads in the opposite direction.[2]

The UK's University College of London, through its Centre for the Study of the Legacies of British Slavery (LBS), published a series of findings that revealed the scale of the economic impact of slavery. The findings included previously unseen records of those who had owned slaves who received a payout from the government when slavery was abolished. Dr. Nick Draper revealed that as many as one-fifth of Victorian Britons' wealth stemmed from the lucrative slave trade and many of these families remain rich today. For example, a certain John Austin owned 415 enslaved and was awarded £20,511 when slavery was abolished, which in today's money is £17 million. In fact, the British paid out some £20 million to 3,000 families who owned slaves for their "loss of property." This was an astonishing 40% of the country's annual budget, and in today's money this equates to £16.5 billion. And if one ever doubted the relationship between wealth and social mobility, some of those whose families received compensation are former business owners, government ministers, and even prime ministers.

Haiti won its independence from France in 1804. Then known as Saint-Domingue, it should have been an inspiration to other enslaved nations. It was a nation of free Black slaves who had won their independence. But it was also seen as a threat, because it might inspire other slave revolts. Under Thomas Jefferson, the United States economically and diplomatically isolated Haiti. But the French took an even more direct approach. Through the threat of war that Haiti was ill-equipped to win, France demanded Haiti pay 150 million francs to secure its independence. This is the equivalent of between $20 billion and $30 billion in today's dollars. It took Haiti 122 years to pay it off.[3]

In the United States, a movement called the National Coalition of Blacks for Reparation (N'COBRA) was formed in 1987. It was headed by individuals such as Walter R. Vaughan, who believed reparations would regenerate the South, and Audley Moore, a prominent Black nationalist leader known as "Queen Mother." Similarly, the National Association for the Advancement of Colored People (NAACP) endorsed reparations in 1993. Yet neither the British nor American government has seriously considered the issue through a bill or piece or legislation. Starting in 1989 and for 25 years, Congressman John Conyers Jr. introduced a bill calling for a congressional study of slavery and its lingering effects as well as recommendations for "appropriate remedies" at every congressional opening. The bill, known as H.R. 40 after "40 acres and a mule," has never made it onto the House floor under either the Democrats or the Republicans.[4]

William Darity and Kirsten Mullen produced arguably the most comprehensive argument for reparations for the Black descendants of slavery to date. In *Here to Equality: Reparations for Black Americans in the Twenty-First Century* (2020), they outline the historical reasons and contemporary case for compensation. Estimates to reduce the racial wealth gap in the United States are $12–14 trillion, but Darity and Mullen argue that during the pandemic, governments mobilized vast sums without commensurate rise in taxes.

They also state that there are precedents for reparations, as demonstrated by the $80 billion paid to Holocaust victims by Germany and then another $662 million announced in 2020. The US Justice Department's Office for Victims of Crime set aside $8.3 million for those who suffered from the Boston Marathon bombing attack. Eligibility should be limited to those who self-identify as African American, Afro-American, or Negro on a legal document in the 12 years before a reparation-study commission or reparations program begins. Darity and Mullen also make the case for indirect payments through a series of programs.

Before we can consider the creation of wealth, the poverty many Black people experience needs to be overcome. Any attempt needs to equip individuals with the ability to control their economic future, like their White counterparts. Universal basic income (UBI) is a government-guaranteed payment made each month to its citizens. This means the basic cost of living is paid for through a flat monthly payment. Some programs envisage a payment being made even if an individual is working and has an income. Proponents of UBI claim it could lift families out of poverty, something traditional welfare programs fail to do. These programs could also be easier and cheaper to administer than current welfare programs and in times of economic stress could help stabilize economies through the maintenance of consumer spending.

This idea often gets lost in ideological arguments. Martin Luther King Jr. was a supporter of UBI. Those on the political right question whether an income program is compatible with capitalism and free market economics. Free income might disincentivize people to find jobs. Some critics also argue the increased spending power could actually cause inflation and recipients will fritter away any funds. But perhaps we need to think about this differently, the ideological arguments being a red herring. The labor market is actually inefficient if swaths of people are out of work and, therefore, unproductive. The other main challenge is the cost of implementing a program. But it requires a costly and inefficient web of government bodies to administer welfare. And to demonstrate the point, UBI had another supporter in shareholder capitalism's biggest advocate, Milton Friedman. Friedman was a vocal advocate of UBI because he felt this was the chief method to lift people out of poverty. He proposed funding it through a negative income tax whereby the poor would receive a tax credit if their income fell below a minimum level. This would be the equivalent to the tax payment for the families earning above the minimum level. Another solution has been proposed by economists Kalle Moene and Debraj Ray. They suggest a system tied to a country's economic output. Their idea is 10 to 12% of GDP going directly to income payments, with levels fluctuating according to economic output. They call this universal basic share.[5]

There are many estimates to fund a UBI program. One UK study puts this at £67 billion per year, or 3.4% of GDP. This net cost of the program of £7,706 for adults and £3,853 for children adds only 39% to the cost of the existing benefit system and an 8.7% increase in the UK total government spending.[6] In a US study, providing every American adult $12,000 per annum would cost the US government $3.1 trillion per year.[7] These figures, however, are for a universal program. While this has merit in its own right, this might not tackle the specific challenges that Black people face. The risk is that if we repeat the policies of Keynes, by attempting to reduce inequality for all, we fail to reduce Black inequity.

Instead, we should consider a guaranteed income program to lift Black families out of poverty that could be even more affordable. Pilot programs have been assessed with encouraging results. In June 2020, the Scottish Citizens' Basic Income Feasibility Study Steering Group produced "Assessing the Feasibility of Citizens Basic Income Pilots in Scotland: Final Report," which concluded a basic income program was desirable to alleviate the poverty many groups in the country faced, particularly after the global pandemic. But the report noted that implementation was a challenge given the current welfare institutional arrangements.

The United States has gone one step further with over 33 guaranteed income programs launched. Former Stockton, California, mayor Michael Tubbs launched the Mayors for a Guaranteed Income network, with over 60 mayors participating and either advocating or launching pilot programs for their residents. Tubbs's program launched in 2019, and the Stockton Economic Empowerment Demonstration (SEED) offered low-income residents hundreds of dollars a month. The program gave 125 randomly selected Stockton residents a 24-month guaranteed income. SEED's hypothesis is that experiences such as poor mental and physical health, unemployment, poor educational attainment, and greater levels of imprisonment or incarceration are symptoms of economic inequality. The results from SEED and other pilot programs are promising. The recipients made rational decisions about the income they received, spending it on necessities such as food, utilities, and car care. The recipients were also able to assist people in their extended networks (i.e., their community), and were able to deal with unexpected expenses. The income also allowed them to spend more time with their families, and children in particular, and members reported improvements in their mental health. The program also resulted in an increase in full-time employment; 28% of the recipients had a full-time job at the beginning of the project, but after one year that had risen to 40%, with some of the individuals citing the ability to retrain, complete a degree, or simply apply for new positions.[8]

The SEED program did not target a specific demographic. Any program should take into account the specific challenges Black communities face. We also need to ensure we have adequate data to implement such a program. This would be difficult to launch in France, for example, because of their "color blind" approach. Nevertheless, there is enough evidence here to warrant further examination. Reducing poverty, however, is just the start. This should be the minimum expectation. To reduce the wealth gap requires tackling a host of other economic hurdles.

For example, we should consider the familial situation of many Black families. A Black child is disadvantaged even before they are born, having inherited the legacy and ongoing discrimination. Investing in a child's future is one such way to level the playing field. One possible solution to this is a "Baby Bond." These are issued by governments and give every child a public-funded trust account that matures upon a child reaching adulthood. One such scheme was trialed in the UK through the Child Trust Fund, a long-term, tax-free savings account for children born between September 1, 2002, and January 2, 2011. The scheme has since been replaced with the junior individual savings account. In the United States, Darity and Mullen helped conceive of the idea. Their research showed that if given only to Black children, the bonds would return an average of £33,333 by early adulthood.[9]

Education should be the next consideration. I attended university between 1997 and 2000 and was fortunate to receive a government-funded grant that did not have to be repaid. If it wasn't for this and my part-time job, I would not have been able to gain a university degree. In both the US and now the UK, university education has to be self-funded, often through very expensive loans. I once gave a talk to some 16–17-year-old students who were considering attending university. They were clearly very bright, but I was constantly asked whether it was necessary to attend university to land a career in finance. I was confused. "Why wouldn't you wish to go to university?" It wasn't until I spoke to one of the schoolteachers that he told me they were worried about leaving university with huge amounts of debt. One answer to this is providing means-tested funding or debt relief, which could ease financial burden on Black students.

Upon graduating university, many Black workers will aspire to buy a home that for many will be their most significant investment. But many suffer from a lack of access to credit or may struggle to build up enough capital for a deposit. In the UK, affordable housing encompasses a range of government-backed schemes designed to provide those who cannot buy housing entry into the private rental market. Those eligible are means tested and are typically from lower-income households.

Darity and Mullen, however, question whether these programs are enough. For example, they estimate that Baby Bonds will reduce the racial wealth gap by just 25%. Financial support for home buying might eliminate the difference in homeownership rates between Whites and Blacks, but it doesn't address the ongoing discriminatory practices in equity values. In the United States, a home in a neighborhood with no Black residents has a median value of $341,000, while homes in a majority Black neighborhood have a median value of $184,000. The value of the equity Whites hold in their homes is $216,000, while for Blacks it's $94,000.[10] In the UK, Black families may be able to get onto the housing ladder through affordable housing schemes, but the value of the properties or the share they own will always lag behind that of the private rental market.

Student-debt relief would help Black students due to their higher-than-average levels of debt but would not address the lower enrollment rates for Black students: 41% for White students when compared to 36% for Black. And after this is factored, student-loan forgiveness yields an average increase in net worth of $8,424 for Blacks and a White increase of $6,560, thus reducing the average gap in Black and White wealth by 1%.[11]

These challenges leave us in a quandary because it's quite clear that no one solution alone can close the racial wealth gap. However, a more joined-up approach across different initiatives could make the difference. A child who receives the proceeds from a Baby Bond and who also receives student debt relief has a better opportunity than one who only has help getting onto the property ladder. We must think about the life journey of an individual and interventions that are necessary throughout someone's life to improve their economic opportunities. The concept is an expanded version of unkinking the hosepipe.

If we can design a model that tracks this, it will not only afford a joined-up approach but will also allow us to assess which interventions have the greatest impact. The hypothesis is that disadvantages resulting from one's race lead to an inequality of opportunity. This in turn leads to inequality of outcome that not only perpetuates inequalities but creates a drag on overall economic growth. Further, interventions that reduce the inequalities of opportunity can break the cycle, create a multiplier effect, and create value.

To quantify the level of opportunity and, hence, inequalities, we need to introduce the concept of advantage. In the model, advantage is quantifiable and calculated as a function of multiple underlying items that reflect access to opportunities. These items might include proximity to good schools, parental health, and income.

The desired outcomes might be increased employment, income, wealth, and a reduction of imprisonment or incarceration. These are outcomes conventionally associated with inequalities in economics. If we can quantify these elements, it might be possible to create an index to use as a benchmark for inequality across not just regions but also geographies. We may be able to understand and mitigate racial inequality in the UK and US, but also in Australia, France, the Caribbean, and then even for other disadvantaged groups. The idea behind the advantage, or Opportunity Index, is based on the notion of assessing factors and their corresponding weights. In economics we call these elasticities. We can devise a unique and effective tool to measure the relative amount of opportunity economic agents possess. This tool should be devised at the micro level, with the potential of generating a macro index.

The first step is to define the index, its constituents, and their weighting. We typically focus on education as the primary driver of life outcomes, but our hypothesis is that there are other factors we should also take into consideration.

Index constituents	Index	Weight
Mother's job	1	sample based
Mother's education	1	sample based
Mother's ethnicity	1	0 – other 1 – White
Father's job	1	sample based
Father's education	1	sample based
Father's ethnicity	1	0 – other 1 – White
Religion born in	1	sample based

Index constituents	Index	Weight
Parents' country	1	0 – other 1 – UK
Gender	2	0 – female 1 – male
Ethnicity – White	3	0 – other 1 – White
Number of siblings	4	sample based
Grandparents' country of birth	5	0 – other 1 – UK
Ethnicity – non-White	6	sample based

The first index is constructed based on factors such as parents' education, ethnicity, and job status, the country parents are born in, and the religion they are affiliated with since birth. The logic behind this stems from the fact that parents define the environment a child is raised in.

Further modifications of the index include gender differences, the effects of grandparents, and, most importantly, the effect of ethnicity beyond just being White versus non-White. Ethnicity is one of the key distinguishing features when it comes to a difference in opportunities among economic agents, and hence great importance was attributed to that feature.

We started with the UK as it allows us to standardize the economic agents. It also afforded access to data with a median sample size to enable us to draw some early conclusions. We also wanted to see the impact of a country that has experienced economic growth but also has stark societal and racial inequalities that impact opportunities.

The preliminary results allowed us to quantify what we suspected and prove our hypothesis. The main conclusions indicate significant effects of opportunity indices on the level of labor income that we measure as net monthly income in US dollars.

It is very important to indicate that the sample we are using is the representative sample of the UK population. The data originate from the 11 data sets of the Understanding Society, which is a part of the British Household Panel.[12] These should also be regarded as preliminary results.

In the graphs, we observe the relationship between the level of income and the Opportunity Index. On the y-axis we have income categories, and on the x-axis we can observe the Opportunity Index and the values observed in the table. These indicate the percentage of people who have a particular level of opportunity within each income category.

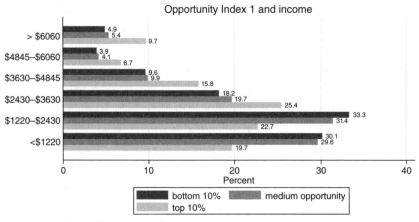

Source: Understanding Society

Racial Composition

Ethnic group	Freq.	Percent	Cum.
Proxy respondent	2486	2.88	2.88
Don't know	11	0.01	2.90
British/English/Scottish/Welsh/ Northern Irish	70158	81.37	84.27
Irish	990	1.15	85.42

Ethnic group	Freq.	Percent	Cum.
Gypsy or Irish Traveler	11	0.01	85.43
Any other White background	2211	2.56	87.99
White and Black Caribbean	539	0.63	88.62
White and Black African	121	0.14	88.76
White and Asian	209	0.24	89.00
Any other mixed background	264	0.31	89.31
Indian	2574	2.99	92.29
Pakistani	1243	1.44	93.74
Bangladeshi	880	1.02	94.76
Chinese	506	0.59	95.34
Any other Asian background	572	0.66	96.01
Caribbean	1353	1.57	97.58
African	1045	1.21	98.79
Any other Black background	121	0.14	98.93
Arabic	143	0.17	99.09
Any other ethnic group	781	0.91	100.00
Total	86218	100.00	

Source: Vojnovic, J., Bowie, D., Lewis, G., British Household Panel Survey, British Understanding Society: The UK Household Longitudinal Study, August 2022, https://www.understandingsociety.ac.uk/about/british-household-panel-survey.

As you can see, 9.7% of individuals who score in the top 10% in Opportunity Index 1 earn more than $6,060 per month, while only 19.7% earn less than $1,220 per month. The drivers of scoring in the top 10% are having White parents born in the UK who are university educated, have a profession, and who belong to the Church of England. This is compared to only 4.9% of those who score in the bottom

10% earning $6,060 per month and 30.1% earning $1220 per month. The drivers of scoring in the bottom 10% are having parents who are non-White, born outside of the UK, and who did not attend university.

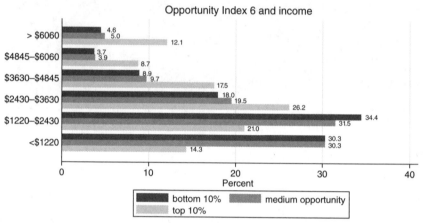

Opportunity Index 6 and income

Source: Understanding Society

Religious Composition

Ethnic group	Freq.	Percent	Cum.
Proxy respondent	2486	2.88	2.88
Don't know	11	0.01	2.90
British/English/Scottish/Welsh/ Northern Irish	70158	81.37	84.27
Irish	990	1.15	85.42
Gypsy or Irish Traveler	11	0.01	85.43
Any other White background	2211	2.56	87.99
White and Black Caribbean	539	0.63	88.62
White and Black African	121	0.14	88.76
White and Asian	209	0.24	89.00
Any other mixed background	264	0.31	89.31

Ethnic group	Freq.	Percent	Cum.
Indian	2574	2.99	92.29
Pakistani	1243	1.44	93.74
Bangladeshi	880	1.02	94.76
Chinese	506	0.59	95.34
Any other Asian background	572	0.66	96.01
Caribbean	1353	1.57	97.58
African	1045	1.21	98.79
Any other Black background	121	0.14	98.93
Arabic	143	0.17	99.09
Any other ethnic group	781	0.91	100.00
Total	86218	100.00	

Source: Vojnovic, J., Bowie, D., Lewis, G., British Household Panel Survey, Understanding Society: The UK Household Longitudinal Study, August 2022, https://www.understandingsociety.ac.uk/about/british-household-panel-survey.

Opportunity Index 6 is the most complete index and also includes gender, whether the individual is White or non-White, number of siblings, grandparents' country of birth, and also ethnicity. Here we can see that 12.1% of individuals who score in the top 10% earn more than $6,060 and only 14.3% earn less than $1,220. The drivers of scoring in the top 10% are having White parents and grandparents who are born in the UK, being White, being male, having parents who attended university, working in a profession, having fewer siblings, and belonging to the Church of England. By contrast, only 4.6% of those who score in the bottom 10% in the Opportunity Index earn more than $6,060, while 30.3% of those who score in the bottom 10% in the Opportunity

Index earn less than \$1,220 per month. The drivers of scoring in the bottom 10% are having parents and grandparents born outside of the UK, who did not attend university, who are non-White, having a more than two siblings, not following a religion, and being an ethnic minority.

The evidence indicates those who score the highest on the scale of opportunity tend to have the highest level of monthly income.

Education is often seen as having the greatest impact on income. But interestingly, when we examine the impact of other variables such as health, religion, and familial structure, these also had a marked effect—much more than we would have envisaged. This demonstrates that we still have much to understand about the drivers of inequality.

From a practical perspective, it should therefore be possible to find "investable" interventions that would enable the levels of advantage to be adjusted and made more equal in a way that will create value for the individuals and also value for those investing to make the changes. Ideally, this will enable instruments to be created that will draw in private investment alongside public money to reduce inequality. The nature of the return on the investment arises from economic growth and reduced societal costs. Successful intervention is likely to need public sector investment but also input from the private sector.[13]

It is also important to note that the framework provides no guarantee of outcome. But what it may do is provide equality of opportunity that can be utilized across a broad range of demographics and jurisdictions.

I have discussed the importance income plays in reducing the wealth gap. But two research economists at the Federal Bank of Cleveland, Dionissi Aliprantis and Daniel Carroll, took this one step further. They argue that the racial wealth gap can be almost entirely explained by the gap in income between Black and White households. Inheritance, such as the proceeds from property, only accounts for 23%.[14] A significant step the private sector can take is to collect and assess data through encouraging employees to self-identify rather than waiting for government legislation. Many firms have found it challenging to gather enough data from their workforce to understand any pay-gap differentials.

We assume that it's the Black employees who are unwilling to self-identify as Black, but there will also be a large proportion of White employees who are also unwilling to self-identify as White. In attempting to create change, whether in the workplace or in society, there will typically be three cohorts:

1. The first are advocates who believe in the rationale for change and are willing proponents; this may be 10–15% of the population who are convinced by the value and beliefs argument for racial equality.
2. Then there are the disengaged who are actively against the change. Again, this may be about 10–15% of the population who don't value or believe in racial equality.
3. The third cohort are the remaining 70–80% who are not particularly for or against but are driven by self-interest and logic. We can try to convince the disengaged, but it is the logical self-interested group that will create the biggest shift. The discussion needs to be put in terms they understand. To a line manager in an organization who adds 35% to the company's bottom line, this makes little difference to their day-to-day activities, but we should also tap into this group's expertise.

Moving the middle may just be as simple as telling them what to do, whether mandated by government or by organizations themselves. But other methods can be employed through creating agency.

The first is moving away from a values or beliefs discussion to a rational evidence-based approach. Understanding the economic impact of entire groups in society underperforming in education, having long-term unemployment, confronting extra judicial interactions, lacking sufficient physical and mental healthcare is an imperative if this issue is to receive the same attention as other risks. In 2020, Citi produced a report that found racial inequality cost the US economy $16 trillion over the last two decades alone.[15] Businesses can establish ways to mitigate this risk as they would any other risk and this becomes less about beliefs or values and more about good business practice. In fact, we already have a way for business to categorize this. Within environment, social, and governance (ESG), the focus on sustainability has ensured the "E" is on the agenda; perhaps it's time to do the same for the "S."

Where there is risk there is opportunity. The same Citi report found that if the racial wealth gap were reduced today, it would add $5 trillion to the US economy over the next five years. A report by the UK consultancy BACKLIGHT found that up to £4.5 billion in disposable income by multi-ethnic consumers is being overlooked by big brands and British businesses.[16]

One of those key drivers according to the report stems from a lack of lending to Black entrepreneurs, which Citi estimates has cost the US $13 trillion in business revenue and 6.1 million new jobs per year. Similarly in the UK, the British Business Bank produced a report that highlighted the lack of investment in minority founders and entrepreneurs. After starting a business, Black business owners have a median turnover of just £25,000, compared to £35,000 for White business owners. And only half of Black entrepreneurs meet their nonfinancial aims, compared to 70% of White business owners. And a report published by the not-for-profit group Extend Ventures revealed that in 2019, only 2% of the £10 billion of venture capital available went to teams that included minority founders. Of these, Black entrepreneurs struggled to gain funding the most. Between 2009 and 2019, 38 Black entrepreneurs received 0.24% of funds available.[17] Lending or investing in minority-owned businesses could also unlock additional revenue to the economy. But the industry should also understand that they have a repository of knowledge, skills, contacts, and expertise to which many minority-owned business do not have access.

One feature of the Opportunity Index must therefore be the assessing of broader risks and opportunities. If we can make this granular enough, a firm can assess the impact to their business. For example, a law firm can offer services to a whole new group of entrepreneurs. Or a supermarket chain can assess the revenue impact of attracting new customers, or losing existing ones, to its business in a given location.

We should also consider the social elements of this solution. It's critical we continue to combat social disadvantage, the work of community activists being paramount. In the workplace, DE&I should continue to focus on attracting but also retaining talent. There are full-time experts who are leading change in this area. We also need to take a hard line on entrenched biases from lending criteria through to computer algorithms. But we should also consider the intersection of economic and social disadvantage. Here, the private sector can be a real engine of change. Together with close friend and client Andrien, I launched a free school program for students attending schools in disadvantaged areas. Andrien manages a pension fund and is also an elected member of the City of London Council. We designed the program to equip students with the skills, knowledge, and aspiration to build a career in finance. But it was also to democratize the education advantages other children might have. The finance industry has some of the brightest minds; entering schools and educational establishments can supplement the work being undertaken by stretched schoolteachers. Providing vocational finance training, work experience, and even sponsoring students from an early age is a social investment. It might open a pipeline of talent and change the perspective of companies. We need to look at initiatives such as these and others and assess the impact they are having against the Opportunity Index.

The investment industry also excels at innovation. Some of this thinking could be applied to some of the unique challenges Black communities face. For example, this could entail working in partnership with governments to find savings solutions. These could be applied across childhood, adulthood, and into retirement. The industry could also work in conjunction with Black business founders and entrepreneurs to plug the funding and access gaps which exist.

Cynics will say this is not profitable, so firms are not incentivized. But it should be seen as part of the solution to reducing the wealth gap that is beneficial to the broader economy. It allows firms to take responsibility for the communities in which they operate. This is not wealth extraction but wealth creation, a move away from rentier capitalism that should be beneficial for all.

At the time of writing, some change is occurring. Many firms are now demanding minority representation at the board and senior levels of the organization before considering investing. In 2021, the US Securities and Exchange Commission (SEC) approved new rules for Nasdaq that require companies that list shares on its exchange to meet certain race and gender targets. In 2016, Sir John Parker led a review of UK board diversity and in its final report urged businesses to improve ethnic and cultural diversity to better reflect their employee base and the communities they serve. A number of recommendations were made, including that each FTSE 100 board have at least one director from an ethnic minority background by 2021 and for each FTSE 250 board to achieve the same by 2024.[18]

The report also recommended a pipeline of candidates and succession plans be instituted through mentoring and sponsorship and greater transparency and disclosure to track progress. Progress has been made, with 89 of the FTSE 100 meeting this by the end of 2021 and 94% of the FTSE 250 having achieved this by May 2022, albeit the majority in nonexecutive director roles.[19] Only six FTSE 100 firms have an ethnically diverse CEO, and none are Black. We are also seeing asset owners beginning to demand increased minority representation from asset managers, while asset managers are demanding increased representation from counterparties and vendors.

In February 2022 the Biden-Harris Administration announced a series of initiatives to create economic opportunities for Black families and communities through family relief, investment in infrastructure, entrepreneurs and small businesses, an end to housing discrimination, and investing in education.[20] The UK government under the leadership of Boris Johnson also pursued an interventionist approach; though this was primarily aimed at regional disparities, its outcome was the reduction of inequality through a program entitled "levelling up." Johnson was succeeded by Prime Minister Liz Truss, who moved away from this interventionist approach and back towards the Thatcherite idea of low taxation as the fuel for growth. These policies however triggered further economic instability and Truss has since been succeeded by Rishi Sunak, Britain's first Asian Prime

Minister. It is expected that Sunk will demonstrate greater fiscal conservatism to restore economic stability.

We should assess the impact of all of these initiatives on inequality and Black communities once embedded.

It's tempting to assume change must come from institutions, but we all have a role to play. There are a host of Black professionals, business groups, activists, and community groups who have been trying to increase opportunities and representation, often quietly and without fanfare. They are also assisted by groups of allies. These are the unsung heroes who sacrifice daily. But they are part of the 10 to 15% who are the advocates; we need to increase these numbers. Here the role of the individual becomes pivotal.

Stephanie and Bastian are close family friends who have two daughters the same age as ours. We both made the decision to send our children to a fee-paying school, but for differing reasons. I was (and, to be honest, still am) in conflict about this. I always felt that two-tier education exacerbates existing inequalities. But my children are female and mixed race. Given how hard it was for me to break through, I felt I needed to give them every chance. When I explained this to Stephanie she was taken aback. "Really? You still think race is an issue?" I didn't bother trying to explain. Fast-forward to the aftermath of the killing of George Floyd, and Stephanie and I had a very different conversation. She now understood that the problem still exists and like many asked what she could do. I pushed back, because I was exhausted from answering the same question, but also because I don't have all the answers. I told Stephanie that she needs to own the solution as much as I do. A few months later we discussed the subject again. Stephanie is a very talented interior designer and has an amazing network of suppliers and contractors she uses to complete her projects. This time the conversation was different; Stephanie had found some Black-owned suppliers and contractors. Most importantly, this added significant value to Stephanie's business by diversifying her suppliers, but it also enabled her to use her platform to make a difference.

Similarly, Carolyn is a colleague with whom I used to work when I first entered the industry. Twenty years ago, discussions about race and gender were taboo, even though we were both minorities of similar age. We had more in common that we realized; we both grew up in single-parent households and didn't really have an obvious route into the industry. But discussing these things was simply not done. After I left the firm, we remained in contact. Carolyn was always supportive of my efforts to increase diversity in the industry, but like many didn't realize that she also had the ability to make a difference. After the events of May 2020 she met a young Black man called Antonay for a coffee; he was in search of some guidance. On the surface they came from very different backgrounds, but Carolyn felt she could at least relate to his experience of gaining access to the industry without any sponsorship or connections. Antonay also had the benefit of being mentored by other individuals and was also selected to participate in a group for high-potential Black students established by Baroness Valerie Amos, a politician and diplomat.

The few senior Black professionals in the finance industry are often inundated with requests to meet and mentor, but given the of number Black leaders relative to our White peers, it's unlikely these young Black entrants will be reporting to a Black person. I've always felt real change will come when White leaders interact with Black talent formally, but crucially informally. Reflecting on her interactions with Antonay, Carolyn felt she learned as much as he did and that although understanding his cultural perspective was difficult, it was OK to discuss Antonay's experience as a young Black male. Antonay won a scholarship to attend university. With his ability and the support from the Black community, he is bound for success. But diversity of input can add to one's chances. Carolyn assisted in his application and marked this as one of the highlights of her career.

EPILOGUE

WHEN I EMBARKED ON THE journey of writing this book, I was determined to take a different approach, and to utilize the skills I had learned through 20 years of working in the business world to solve a problem that has existed for centuries. This meant taking a quantitative as well as qualitative approach. One of the first tasks was therefore to find a measure for inequality. I posed the question to economists, actuaries, and academics. All were stumped. I was shocked that a universally accepted measure doesn't exist. So I forged a small group of equally passionate individuals to create one. Along with a professor of economics and a partner in an actuarial consultancy, we have created a framework that can be used to measure inequality and maximize opportunity. Our hypothesis is that the causes of socioeconomic disadvantage are both social and economic in nature. And by making the correct interventions, we can change life outcomes.

We would like to analyze more data sets to test the strength of the Opportunity Index. Once we establish the relationship in the case of the United Kingdom, we would like to undertake analysis in the other jurisdictions such as the United States and Australia. This plan is formed on the idea that these are countries that have experienced economic growth but still experience inequality.

The Opportunity Index may also enable us to measure the impact of inequality on productivity and economic performance, an area that requires much greater attention. If we can enlist the support of policy makers and institutions, both public and private, we may be able to make a difference to entire segments of society, a win-win and no longer a zero-sum game.

We should also find existing initiatives that are resolving economic inequality. These will enable us to use evidence and measure their outcomes against the Opportunity Index.

We also need to understand the factors behind the drivers for one's score in the Opportunity Index. Is there something inherent in religion that leads to better life outcomes? Or is it the community that often comes alongside it?

Writing this book presented both a physical and an emotional challenge. I began writing after a very difficult period, but this enabled me to express emotions I would have otherwise internalized. I then continued writing in the midst of a global pandemic, racial upheaval, and, more recently, war and a cost-of-living crisis. I did this while trying to be the best father, husband, and friend I could be. I'm not sure I always got the balance right. I also had to revisit some painful memories and recount these experiences. I discovered where my journey really started and why at times progressing felt impossible.

This does, however, seem like watershed moment. I believe I have a better understanding of my own circumstances and that of the wider Black community. I also feel I have purpose. A sense of direction. When everything feels almost too much, this provides a reservoir of energy I am able to dip into. I have a platform to make a difference, and I now know how to use it.

Whether you feel I have told your story or whether this is entirely new, I hope this has made a difference to you.

I see the opportunity. I hope you do too.

ENDNOTES

INTRODUCTION

1. Corporation of London, City of London Resident Population Census 2001, July 2005.
2. Shalchi, A., Georgina Hutton, and M. Ward, Financial services: contribution to the UK economy, December 8. 2021, https://commonslibrary.parliament.uk/research-briefings/sn06193/.
3. Look Up London, Gargoyles of Gracechurch Street, May 26, 2020, https://lookup.london/51-54-gracechurch-street/.
4. Monument: Gilt of Cain, London Remembers, https://www.londonremembers.com/memorials/gilt-of-cain-slave-trade.
5. Wolffe, J., William Wilberforce (1759–1833), WikiTree, May 21, 2009, https://www.wikitree.com/wiki/Wilberforce-2.
6. Wall Street, *Encyclopaedia Britannica*, https://www.britannica.com/topic/Wall-Street-New-York-City.

7. New York City Slave Market, New York Public Library, June 29, 2015, https://www.nypl.org/blog/2015/06/29/slave-market.
8. New York City Council approves monument to slaves, BBC, April 16, 2015, https://www.bbc.com/news/world-us-canada-32340683.
9. Lewis, T., Transatlantic Slave Trade, History & Facts, *Encyclopedia Britannica*, https://www.britannica.com/topic/transatlantic-slave-trade.
10. Hedman, M., F. E. Folatomi, N. Okukenu, and P. Boateng, Inequality Risk: The Black British Wealth Creation Report, November 2, 2021, https://www.voice-online.co.uk/news/sponsored-news/2021/11/02/black-britain-and-beyond-release-inequality-risk-the-black-british-wealth-creation-report/.

CHAPTER 1

1. The Royal Exchange, Guildhall Library blog, August 28, 2020, https://guildhalllibrarynewsletter.wordpress.com/2020/08/28/the-royal-exchange/.
2. Ibid.
3. The Royal Exchange, Symbols & Secrets, October 18, 2018, https://symbolsandsecrets.london/2018/10/18/the-royal-exchange/.
4. The History of Jamaica, Jamaica Information Service, May 30, 2022, https://jis.gov.jm/information/jamaican-history/.
5. Ibid.
6. Ibid.
7. Jacobs, Harriet, *Incidents in the Life of a Slave Girl*, 1861.
8. Britain and the Slave Trade, National Archives, 2022, https://www.nationalarchives.gov.uk/.
9. Hakim, A., Africa and the Transatlantic Slave Trade, October 5, 2012, chrome-extension://efaidnbmnnnibpcajpcglclefindmkaj/https://www.tradingfacesonline.com/docs/voices/pdf/Transatlantic_Essay.pdf.

10. Clarke, C. G., and B. M. Brereton, Colonialism of the West Indies, *Encyclopaedia Britannica*, https://www.britannica.com/place/West-Indies-island-group-Atlantic-Ocean/Colonialism.
11. Joseph E. Inikori, The Volume of the British Slave Trade, 1655–1807, *African Studies Notebooks*, 1992.
12. Lex in depth, Examining the slave trade – Britain has a debt to repay, *Financial Times*, June 28, 2020, https://www.ft.com/content/945c6136-0b92-41bf-bd80-a80d944bb0b8.
13. Rice, A., The economic basis of the slave trade, Revealing Histories, 2007, http://revealinghistories.org.uk/africa-the-arrival-of-europeans-and-the-transatlantic-slave-trade/articles/the-economic-basis-of-the-slave-trade.html.
14. Ibid.
15. University College London, Centre for the Study of the Legacies of British Slavery, 2022, https://www.ucl.ac.uk/lbs/.
16. Slavery in America, History.com, May 19, 2022, https://www.history.com/topics/black-history/slavery.
17. The Transatlantic Slave Trade, Lloyds, 2022, https://www.lloyds.com/about-lloyds/history/the-trans-atlantic-slave-trade.
18. Levantine Heritage Foundation, 2015.
19. Pepys, S., *The Diary of Samuel Pepys*, Monday December 10, 1660.
20. Ibid., Thursday September 7, 1665.
21. The History of the Tontine, Tontine Trust, October 10, 2019, https://tontine.com/news/news-tontinehistory.
22. Gordon, G.S., Constituting America, May 17, 1792: The Buttonwood Agreement and the New York Stock Exchange, August 6, 2022, https://constitutingamerica.org/may-17-1792-the-buttonwood-agreement-and-the-new-york-stock-exchange-guest-essayist-john-steele-gordon/.
23. Tardi, C. Tontine, Investopedia, May 28, 2021, https://www.investopedia.com/terms/t/tontine.asp.

24. DeMatos, D., TCH: The Tontine Coffee-House, October 15, 2018, https://tontinecoffeehouse.com/2018/10/15/the-tontine-coffee-house/.
25. Beckert, S., Empire of Cotton, *The Atlantic,* December 12, 2014, https://www.theatlantic.com/business/archive/2014/12/empire-of-cotton/383660/.
26. Largest stock exchange operators worldwide, Statista_Research Department, 2022, https://www.statista.com/statistics/270126/largest-stock-exchange-operators-by-market-capitalization-of-listed-companies/.
27. Smith, A., *The Wealth of Nations,* March 9, 1776.
28. Juneteenth and the Broken Promise of the "40 Acres and a Mule," National Farmers Union, June 19, 2020, https://nfu .org/2020/06/19/juneteenth-and-the-broken-promise-of-40-acres-and-a-mule/.

CHAPTER 2

1. Marshall. K., The Black Dollar Doesn't Circulate Like It Should, The Famuan, October 1, 2020, http://www.thefamuanonline.com/2020/10/01/the-black-dollar-doesnt-circulate-like-it-should/.
2. Thibert, K., O.W. Gurley (1868–1935), blackpast.org, September 19, 2020, https://www.blackpast.org/african-american-history/o-w-gurley-1868-1935/.
3. Montford, C., 6 Interesting Things You Didn't Know About "Black Wall Street," *Atlanta Black Star*, December 2, 2014.
4. Khan, O., The Colour of Money, Runnymede Report, 2020, https://www.runnymedetrust.org/publications/the-colour-of-money.
5. McIntosh, K., E. Moss, R. Nunn, and J. Shambaugh, Examining the Black-White wealth gap, Brookings, February 27, 2020, https://www.brookings.edu/blog/up-front/2020/02/27/examining-the-black-white-wealth-gap/.

6. Newkirk II, V. R., The Great Land Robbery, *Atlantic,* September 2019, https://www.theatlantic.com/magazine/archive/2019/09/ this-land-was-our-land/594742/.

7. Juneteenth and Broken Promise of "40 acres and a Mule," National Farmers Union, June 19, 2020, https://nfu.org/2020/ 06/19/juneteenth-and-the-broken-promise-of-40-acres-and-a-mule/.

8. What Is the Origin of the Term "Jim Crow"? *Encyclopaedia Britannica,* https://www.britannica.com/story/what-is-the-origin-of-the-term-jim-crow.

9. Civil Rights Act of 1875, *Encyclopaedia Britannica,* https://www .britannica.com/topic/Civil-Rights-Act-United-States-1875.

10. Urofsky, M.I., Civil Rights Cases, *Encyclopedia Britannica,* https://www.britannica.com/topic/Civil-Rights-Cases.

11. Plessy v. Ferguson, *Encyclopedia Britannica,* https://www .britannica.com/event/Plessy-v-Ferguson-1896.

12. 1921 Tulsa Race Massacre, Tulsa Historical Society and Museum, https://www.tulsahistory.org/exhibit/1921-tulsa-race-massacre/.

13. Tulsa Race Massacre, History, May 24, 2022, https://www .history.com/topics/roaring-twenties/tulsa-race-massacre.

14. Ray, M., Emmett Till, *Encyclopedia Britannica,* https://www .britannica.com/biography/Emmett-Till.

15. Rosa Parks, *Encyclopedia Britannica,* https://www.britannica .com/biography/Rosa-Parks.

16. Modern Latin America: Puerto Rico's Operation Bootstrap, Brown University Library, June 25, 2022, https://library.brown .edu/create/modernlatinamerica/chapters/chapter-12-strategies-for-economic-developmen/puerto-ricos-operation-bootstrap/.

17. Puerto Rico Balance of Trade, Trading Economics, May 2022.

18. Poverty in Puerto Rico to be Reduced, Puerto Rico Report, March 26, 2022, https://www.puertoricoreport.com/poverty-in-puerto-rico-to-be-reduced-studies-say/#.YztNnnbMLSI.

19. The History of Jamaica, Jamaica Information Service, 2020, https://jis.gov.jm/information/jamaican-history/.

20. Moyne Commission, Encyclopedia of African-American Culture and History, Encyclopedia.com, August 2, 2022, https://www.encyclopedia.com/history/encyclopedias-almanacs-transcripts-and-maps/moyne-commission.
21. Trade balance of goods of Jamaica 2020, Statista, March 2, 2020, https://www.statista.com/statistics/527173/trade-balance-of-jamaica/.
22. Return to Paradise: A Poverty Perspective on Jamaica's COVID-19 recovery response, World Bank Blogs, November 17, 2020, https://blogs.worldbank.org/latinamerica/return-paradise-poverty-perspective-jamaicas-covid-19-recovery-response.

CHAPTER 3

1. Romer, C.D., and R.H. Pells, Great Depression, *Encyclopedia Britannica*, https://www.britannica.com/event/Great-Depression.
2. Brave New World, Welfare State, National Archives, https://www.nationalarchives.gov.uk/cabinetpapers/alevelstudies/welfare-state.htm.
3. Eichengreen, B., ed., *Europe's Post-War Recovery*, Cambridge University Press, September 7, 2010.
4. New Deal, *Encyclopedia Britannica*, https://www.britannica.com/event/New-Deal.
5. Freidel, F., Franklin D. Roosevelt, *Encyclopedia Britannica*, https://www.britannica.com/biography/Franklin-D-Roosevelt.
6. Servicemen's Readjustment Act (1944), National Archives, https://www.archives.gov/milestone-documents/servicemens-readjustment-act.
7. How British-Caribbeans started the first credit union in Britain, Mutual Interest Media, March 11, 2020, https://www.mutualinterest.coop/2020/03/how-british-caribbeans-started-the-first-credit-union-in-britain.

8. Greenberg, C.L., *To Ask for an Equal Chance: African Americans in the Great Depression*, Rowman & Littlefield, 2009.

9. African Americans in the Great Depression and New Deal, Oxford Research Encyclopedia, November 19, 2020, https:// doi.org/10.1093/acrefore/9780199329175.013.632.

10. Department of Veterans Affairs, Minority Veterans Report, March 2017, chrome-extension://efaidnbmnnnibpcajpcglclefin dmkaj/https://www.va.gov/vetdata/docs/SpecialReports/ Minority_Veterans_Report.pdf.

11. Blakemore, E., How the GI Bill's Promise Was Denied to a Million Black WWII Veterans, History, April 20, 2021, https:// www.history.com/news/gi-bill-black-wwii-veterans-benefits.

12. Powell, E., *Freedom and Reality*, 1969.

13. Bar-Zohar, M., David Ben-Gurion, *Encyclopedia Britannica*, https://www.britannica.com/biography/David-Ben-Gurion.

14. Bristol's Paul Stephenson, *Bristol Post*, November 7, 2017, https://www.bristolpost.co.uk/news/bristol-news/paul-stephenson-bristol-civil-rights-698560.

15. Greensboro Sit-In, History, January 25, 2022, https://www .history.com/topics/black-history/the-greensboro-sit-in.

16. Getchell, M., The Civil Rights Act of 1964 and the Voting Rights Act of 1965, Khan Academy, 2022, https://www .khanacademy.org/humanities/us-history/postwarera/civil-rights-movement/a/the-civil-rights-act-of-1964-and-the-voting-rights-act-of-1965.

17. Equal Educational Opportunities Act, 1973–1974, Congress. gov, August 6, 2022.

18. UK Parliament, 1968 Race Relations Act, https://www.legisla-tion.gov.uk/ukpga/1968/71/enacted.

19. Martin, T., The Beginning of Labor's End? Britain's "Winter of Discontent" and Working-Class Women's Activism, *International Labor and Working-Class History* 75 (2009): 49–67, http://www.jstor.org/stable/27673141.

CHAPTER 4

1. Ronald Reagan. *Encyclopedia Britannica,* https://www.britannica .com/biography/Ronald-Reagan.
2. Young, H., Margaret Thatcher, *Encyclopedia Britannica,* https:// www.britannica.com/biography/Margaret-Thatcher.
3. Martin, T., The Beginning of Labor's End? Britain's "Winter of Discontent" and Working-Class Women's Activism, *International Labor and Working-Class History* 75 (2009): 49–67, http://www.jstor.org/stable/27673141.
4. Steele, J., Last of the old-style liberals, *Guardian,* April 6, 2002, https://www.theguardian.com/education/2002/apr/06/ socialsciences.highereducation.
5. Niskanen, W.A., Reaganomics, *The Concise Encyclopedia of Economics,* 2002.
6. Jones, J., Margaret Thatcher in six graphs, *Spectator,* April 10, 2013.
7. Pettinger, T., 2022, Economicshelp.org.
8. Jones, Margaret Thatcher in six graphs.
9. Rossinow, D., *The Reagan Era: A History of the 1980s,* Columbia University Press, 2015.
10. US Census Bureau, Current Population Survey, 1968–1999, https://www.census.gov/programs-surveys/cps.html.
11. Depository Institutions Deregulation and Monetary Control Act of 1980, Federal Reserve History, November 22, 2013, https://www.federalreservehistory.org/essays/monetary-control-act-of-1980.
12. Kenton, W., Big Bang, Investopedia, June 30, 2022, https:// www.investopedia.com/terms/b/bigbang.asp.
13. Schwartz D.B., How America's Ugly History of Segregation Changed the Meaning of the Word "Ghetto," *Time,* September 24, 2019.
14. Amenity, Oxford Languages, 2022.

CHAPTER 5

1. American Registry, June 2001.
2. Hayes, A., Game Theory, Investopedia, February 2, 2022, https://www.investopedia.com/terms/g/gametheory.asp.
3. Kenton W., Zero-Sum Game, Investopedia, March 20 2022, https://www.investopedia.com/terms/z/zero-sumgame.asp.
4. Stella Dadzie, British Library, 2022, https://www.bl.uk/people/stella-dadzie.
5. Pilgrim, D., The Coon Caricature, Ferris State University, 2012, https://www.ferris.edu/HTMLS/news/jimcrow/coon/homepage.htm.
6. Mathers, M., Stephen Lawrence murder: A timeline of events, *Independent,* August 25, 2021, https://www.independent.co.uk/news/uk/home-news/stephen-lawrence-murder-timeline-events-b1908402.html.
7. Broadwater Farm Riots: PC Keith Blakelock's 1985 murder recalled, BBC, October 6, 2015, https://www.bbc.com/news/uk-england-london-34433752.
8. What caused the 1985 Tottenham Broadwater Farm riot? BBC, March 3, 2014, https://www.bbc.com/news/uk-england-london-26362633.
9. Shielded from Justice: Police Brutality and Accountability in the United States, Human Rights Watch, July 1, 1998, https://www.hrw.org/report/1998/07/01/shielded-justice/police-brutality-and-accountability-united-states.
10. Rashawn, R., and A.W. Galston, Did the 1994 crime bill cause mass incarceration? Brookings, August 28, 2020, https://www.brookings.edu/blog/fixgov/2020/08/28/did-the-1994-crime-bill-cause-mass-incarceration/.
11. 2020 Census Results, US Census, https://www.census.gov/programs-surveys/decennial-census/decade/2020/2020-census-results.html.

CHAPTER 6

1. Holland, K., Amygdala Hijack: When Emotion Takes Over, Healthline, September 17, 2021, https://www.healthline.com/health/stress/amygdala-hijack.
2. Ibid.
3. Ethnicity facts and figures, Gov.uk, June 21, 2021, https://www.ethnicity-facts-figures.service.gov.uk/.
4. Fox, J., Homicide Is Pandemic's Biggest Killer of Young Black Men, Bloomberg, February 22, 2022, https://www.bloomberg.com/opinion/articles/2022-02-22/pandemic-murder-wave-fell-most-heavily-on-young-black-men?leadSource=uverify%20wall.
5. Chronic stress puts your health at risk, Mayo Clinic, July 8, 2021, https://www.mayoclinic.org/healthy-lifestyle/stress-management/in-depth/stress/art-20046037.
6. Yehuda, R., Lehrner, A., Intergenerational transmission of trauma effects: putative role of epigenetic mechanisms, *World Psychiatry* 17 (October 2018): 243–257, doi: 10.1002/wps.20568.
7. MailOnline, March 5, 2019, https://www.dailymail.co.uk/home/sitemaparchive/day_20190305.html.
8. Violence Reduction Unit, 2022, https://www.london.gov.uk/programmes-strategies/mayors-office-policing-and-crime/governance-and-decision-making/mopac-decisions-0/violence-reduction-unit-vru-2022-2023-funding-programme.
9. Flanders-Stepans, M.B., Alarming racial differences in maternal mortality, *Journal of Perinatal Education* 9(Spring 2000): 50–51, doi: 10.1624/105812400X87653.
10. Kovacevic, R., Mental Health: lessons in 2020 for 2021, World bank Blogs, February 11, 2021, https://blogs.worldbank.org/health/mental-health-lessons-learned-2020-2021-and-forward.

11. Mental health matters: Global Health, *Lancet,* November 1, 2020, doi: https://doi.org/10.1016/S2214-109X(20)30432-0.
12. Bauer, A., M. Knapp, and M. Parsonage, Lifetime costs of perinatal anxiety and depression, *Journal of Affective Disorders* 192 (2016): 83–90, https://doi.org/10.1016/j.jad.2015.12.005.
13. Mental health matters: Global Health.
14. Annual Report, Prevention United, 2020–2021, chrome-extension://efaidnbmnnnibpcajpcglclefindmkaj/https://preventionunited.org.au/wp-content/uploads/2021/12/Annual-Report-2020_2021.pdf.

CHAPTER 7

1. Hall, M., The Greatest Wealth Transfer in History: What's happening and what are the implications? *Forbes,* November 11, 2019, https://www.forbes.com/sites/markhall/2019/11/11/the-greatest-wealth-transfer-in-history-whats-happening-and-what-are-the-implications/?sh=24e23a664090.
2. Melling, C., What are the real implications of intergenerational wealth transfer? FTAdvisor, April 27, 2021, https://www.ftadviser.com/investments/2021/04/27/what-are-the-real-implications-of-intergenerational-wealth-transfer/.
3. Ibid.
4. Logan, M.P., On Culture: Edward B. Tylor's Primitive Culture, 1871, July 2012, https://branchcollective.org/?ps_articles=peter-logan-on-culture-edward-b-tylors-primitive-culture-1871.

CHAPTER 8

1. Regional ethnic diversity, Gov.uk, August 1, 2018, https://www.ethnicity-facts-figures.service.gov.uk/uk-population-by-ethnicity/national-and-regional-populations/regional-ethnic-diversity/latest.

2. Our role in London, City of London Corporation, March 17, 2022, https://www.cityoflondon.gov.uk/about-us/about-the-city-of-london-corporation/our-role-in-london; US Census Bureau, Census, April 1, 2020, https://www.census.gov/programs-surveys/decennial-census/decade/2020/2020-census-results.html.

3. Localize. City, July 2021, https://www.localize.city/nyc/.

4. Savage, M., *Social Class in the 21st Century,* Pelican, 2015.

5. Wilkerson, I., *Caste: The Origins of Our Discontent,* Random House, 2020.

6. Oceanic languages, *Encyclopedia Britannica,* https://www.britannica.com/topic/Oceanic-languages.

7. Villiers, A., James Cook, *Encyclopaedia Britannica*, https://www.britannica.com/biography/James-Cook.

8. Multicultural communities, City of Melbourne, August 6, 2022, https://www.melbourne.vic.gov.au/about-melbourne/melbourne-profile/multicultural-communities/Pages/multicultural-communities.aspx.

9. Climate and Average Weather Year Round in Sydney, WeatherSpark, July 15, 2022, https://weatherspark.com/.

10. Ibid.

11. The Stolen Generations, Australians Together, June 15, 2022, https://australianstogether.org.au/discover-and-learn/our-history/stolen-generations.

12. Harjanto, L., and J. Batalova, Vietnamese Immigrants in the United States, Migration Policy Institute, August 25, 2014, https://www.migrationpolicy.org/article/vietnamese-immigrants-united-states.

13. Alperin, E., and J. Batalova, Vietnamese Immigrants in the United States, Migration Policy Institute, September 13, 2018, https://www.migrationpolicy.org/article/vietnamese-immigrants-united-states-5.

14. Tribalat, M. (2015). An estimation of the foreign-origin populations of France in 2011, *Espace, Populations, Sociétés,* July 2015, doi: 10.4000/eps.6073.

15. Braniff, A., Marseille Drug War Escalates to Include Child Victims, September 8, 2021, https://impakter.com/marseille-drug-war-escalates-to-include-child-victims/.

CHAPTER 9

1. Afzal, N., Black people dying in police custody should surprise no one, *Guardian,* January 11, 2020, https://www.theguardian.com/uk-news/2020/jun/11/black-deaths-in-police-custody-the-tip-of-an-iceberg-of-racist-treatment.
2. Schwartz, G.L., and J.L. Jahn, Mapping fatal police violence across U.S. metropolitan areas: Overall rates and racial/ethnic inequities, 2013–2017, *PLOS One,* June 24, 2020, https://doi.org/10.1371/journal.pone.0229686.
3. Munro, André, Shooting of Trayvon Martin. *Encyclopedia Britannica,* https://www.britannica.com/event/shooting-of-Trayvon-Martin.
4. Edwards, J., Obama says Black Lives Matter movement raises "legitimate issue," Reuters, October 22, 2015, https://www.reuters.com/article/us-obama-discrimination/obama-says-black-lives-matter-movement-raises-legitimate-issue-idUSKCN0SG2QM20151022.

CHAPTER 10

1. Royall, Belinda, Slavery and Remembrance: A Guide to Sites, Museums, and Memory, 2022, https://slaveryandremembrance.org/people/person/?id=PP019.
2. Hardin, W., Robert Pleasants (1723–1801), Encyclopedia Virginia, Virginia Humanities, https://encyclopediavirginia.org/entries/pleasants-robert-1723-1801/.
3. Rosalsky, G., "The Greatest Heist in History": How Haiti was Forced to Pay Reparations for Freedom, NPR Planet Money,

October 5, 2021, https://www.npr.org/sections/money/2021/10/05/1042518732/-the-greatest-heist-in-history-how-haiti-was-forced-to-pay-reparations-for-freed.

4. Introduction: What is H.R.-40? Reparations4Slavery, July 18, 2020, https://reparations4slavery.com/hr-40-the-national-reparations-movement/.

5. Moene, O.K., and D. Ray, The universal basic share and social incentives, September 30, 2016, https://www.ideasforindia.in/topics/poverty-inequality/the-universal-basic-share-and-social-incentives.html.

6. Widerquist, K., The Cost of a Full Basic Income for the United Kingdom Would be £67 billion per year (3.4% of GDP), Basic Income Earth Network, September 5, 2020, https://basicincome.org/news/2020/09/the-cost-of-a-full-basic-income-for-the-united-kingdom-would-be-67-billion-per-year-3-4-of-gdp/.

7. Vesoulis, A., and A. Abrams, Inside the Nation's Largest Guaranteed Income Experiment, *Time,* September 16, 2021, https://time.com/6097523/compton-universal-basic-income/.

8. Stockton Economic Empowerment Demonstration, July 19, 2022, https://www.stocktondemonstration.org/.

9. Darity, William, and A. Kirsten Mullen on direct payments to close the racial-wealth gap, *Economist,* May 18, 2021, https://www.economist.com/by-invitation/2021/05/18/william-darity-and-a-kirsten-mullen-on-direct-payments-to-close-the-racial-wealth-gap.

10. Ibid.

11. Ibid.

12. Understanding Society, British Household Panel Survey, August 7, 2022, https://www.understandingsociety.ac.uk/documentation/mainstage/survey-timeline.

13. Vojnovic, J., D. Bowie, and G. Lewis, British Household Panel Survey, Understanding Society: The UK Household Longitudinal Study, August 2022, https://www.understandingsociety.ac.uk/about/british-household-panel-survey.

14. Aliprantis, D., and D.R. Carroll, What Is Behind the Persistence of the Racial Wealth Gap? February 28, 2019, *Economic Commentary* (Federal Reserve Bank of Cleveland), 1–6. doi: 10.26509/frbc-ec-201903.

15. Peterson, D.M., and L.C. Mann, Closing the Racial Inequality Gaps: The Economic Cost of Black Inequality in the US, Citi GPS, September 2020, https://www.citivelocity.com/citigps/closing-the-racial-inequality-gaps/.

16. Amoah, L., Black Pound Report, January 2022, https://www.lydiaamoah.com/the-black-pound-report.

17. Brodnock, E., Diversity Beyond Gender, The State of the Nation for Diverse Entrepreneurs, Extend Ventures, November 2020, chrome-extension://efaidnbmnnnibpcajpcglclefindmkaj/https://www.extend.vc/_files/ugd/52d2fc_1b4c9ee497fb437d99facdc7ed847083.pdf.

18. Parker, J., A Report into the Ethnic Diversity of UK Boards, The Parker Review Committee, October 31, 2017, https://www.addleshawgoddard.com/en/insights/insights-briefings/2017/employment/employment-up-to-date-october-2017/the-parker-review-a-report-into-the-ethnic-diversity-of-uk-boards/.

19. Parker, J., Improving the Ethnic Diversity of UK Boards: An update report from the Parker Review, March 16, 2022, chrome-extension://efaidnbmnnnibpcajpcglclefindmkaj/https://assets.ey.com/content/dam/ey-sites/ey-com/en_uk/topics/diversity/ey-what-the-parker-review-tells-us-about-boardroom-diversity.pdf.

20. Remarks by President Biden at a Celebration to Mark Black History Month WH.gov, February 28, 2022, https://www.whitehouse.gov/briefing-room/speeches-remarks/2022/02/28/remarks-by-president-biden-at-a-celebration-to-mark-black-history-month/.

REFERENCES

Coard, B. *How the Caribbean Child Is Made Educationally Sub-normal in the British School System: The Scandal of the Black Child in Schools in Britain,* 1971.

Eltis, D. *The Rise of African Slavery in the Americas,* 2000.

Fanon, F. *Black Skin, White Masks,* 1952.

Fanon, F. *The Wretched of the Earth,* 1961.

Fukuyama, F. *Thymos,* 2014.

Hegel, F. W. *The Phenomenology of Spirit,* 1807.

Hegel, F. F. *Elements of the Philosophy of Right,* 1820.

Jacobs, Harriet. *Incidents in the Life of a Slave Girl,* 1861.

Jordan, D. W. *White Over Black: American Attitudes Toward the Negro, 1550–1812,* 1968.

Keynes, M. J. *A Treatise on Money,* 1930.

Keynes, M. J. *The General Theory of Employment Interest and Money,* 1936.

Khan, O. *The Colour of Money,* Runnymede, 2020.

King, M. L. *Where Do We Go From Here: Chaos or Community?* 1967.

Parker, J. "A Report into the Ethnic Diversity of UK Boards," The Parker Review Committee, 2017.

Parker, J. "Improving the Ethnic Diversity of UK Boards," Parker Review Committee, 2022.

Pepys, S. *The Diary of Samuel Pepys,* 1660–1665.

Peterson, M. D., and C. L. Mann, "Closing the Racial Inequality Gaps: The Economic Cost of Black Inequality in the U.S.," Citi GPS, September 2020.

Rosenthal, R., and L. Jacobson. *Pygmalion in the Classroom,* 1968.

Taylor, C. *Multiculturalism and "The Politics of Recognition,"* 1992.

Wilkerson, I. *Caste: The Origins of Our Discontent,* Random House, 2020.

Williams, E. *Capitalism & Slavery,* Random House, 1944.

ABOUT THE AUTHOR

GAVIN LEWIS IN AN INVESTMENT professional with 20 years' experience. He is managing director at BlackRock and a cofounder of #Talkaboutblack and sits on the board of the NFL UK Foundation, the Old Vic Theatre, and the Pensions Policy Institute. He holds a degree in history and politics from Queen Mary, University of London.

INDEX

213